Why don't all deceased send messages ?

Measurments.

Car accident Sam. How can

What does the Church to

What research. Where studied

IS THAT YOU?

A mystical scientific investigative journey beyond this life

Sir Oliver Lodge

by Gaye Wilson-Smart

They want us to know they still exist.
Why cannot all communicate

First published in 2011
by Twinlight Books
gayesmart@yahoo.com

With great thanks to all who have contributed especially: Debbie, Annie, Nigel, Rodney, Margaret, Pamela, Dee, Michael, Anitra, Kerry, and so many more but, crucially, to Peter without whom this discovery could not have happened.

The cover is a photo of Peter, taken by Stephanie,
six months **before** he died.

Chapters to take you into the after life world

Chapter One

LIFE *After* DEATH

`Please, can you, or somebody, anybody, tell me how contact can be made with us AFTER someone has died? `

Eighteen year old Sam is pleading with me through intensely blue eyes. He has sandy blonde hair, is tall and slim but he is wearing a look of absolute confusion.

Why has he come to me? You ask. Who am I? Come to that HOW am I qualified to answer this enormous question which ultimately will be of concern to every one of us?

It is because it has **happened to me!**

When my husband died, a little over a year ago, I had no expectation of his ever being in contact with me again. **Yet it was a mere six hours later that his contact with me began. .. directly from a new and different state of existence entirely!**

Since that time Peter has used so many clues, evidence and different ways and means of connecting with my energy. All of which have absolutely convinced me that we DO all continue to exist once we have died from the physical body.

THIS BOOK WILL NOW BECOME AN INVESTIGATION INTO THE WHOLE AFTER LIFE SITUATION TO DISCOVER HOW CONTACT HAPPENS. Every and any question for which either Sam, or myself, need an answer now comes through from the other side

`So why are YOU asking this question, Sam?

Sam: My Dad died, a while ago, and yet he still seems able to keep contacting me and making paranormal things happen.

But how can he do this? How can it be him? He died right in front of me, slipped out of life and just left behind this cold empty shell of a body. Now I have so many questions like:

DOES HE STILL EXIST IN SOME SHAPE OR FORM SOMEWHERE? IF SO WHERE?

And how CAN he be able to move things around, what kind of energy does he have ~ where he is now ~ to do this? *There`s much more I need to know like: do these strange inexplicable things happen to other people too?*

Yes they do, Sam, but give me an idea of his ways of contact.

Sam: Okay well my phone gets up and moves itself into another room, lights flicker, turn themselves off and on and I see flashes of light shooting past me. Sometimes I hear Dad`s voice and I SEE HIM, but how can this be him?

You and I, in fact all of us need answers to this and every other vital question about life after we die. We think these questions can`t be answered but they can, Sam! This is just the right time for us to delve into this whole vast subject.

We hear about people passing over to the other side of life but what do they mean by this? We all need to know. And since I have direct contact with a soul who is now `there`, I`m well placed to bring you the answers. Also a great number of people have shared with me their own experiences of contact with those who have died, and now I can pass them on.

Two intuitive mediums are ready to step forward and reveal their own points of contact with those `on the other side`. Exceptional healers, too, now come through to explain healing abilities which come from another level of energy entirely.

This has to be the right time and place to open up this whole subject in a way that can help and reassure so many people.

And, from here, those already existing in an `other` world of energy will demonstrate and prove their existence to help our investigation, accompanying us as we walk into different energy dimensions, Sam, to explore other parallel worlds.

We can take a journey into realms of history to learn more of the ancient view of death from the Egyptian and Druidic point of view. You`ll be hearing what various monuments of the past have to say about death, life and resurrection

We can ask an eighteenth century Baron exactly what he was doing when he uncovered the secret hidden force of energy which holds the ability to make objects move in our reality.

Be prepared for a fascinating journey, Sam, as we uncover **how** paranormal phenomena happen and **why and where** after life contact can be made. We`ll travel into quantum worlds of physics to unravel universal laws involving resonance, neutrons, photons, electricity and electromagnetic energy for the secret sciences to reveal fundamental truths.

Sam: Hold on, I`ve never been any good at physics or science

Then I`m now asking you to agree that if there`s anything you don`t understand, immediately, you will ask the right questions to make the whole subject accessible for everybody.

Our research will explore the evidence of how death of the physical body never can, never will be the complete and absolute ending of an individual`s core energy.

My husband describes how it feels to die, what lies beyond and how this other parallel invisible world ~ where he is now ~ constantly interacts with our reality.

By walking into *his* world we gain access to universal memory banks to explain how and why seemingly impossible things can and do happen, and we begin to see how the invisible can suddenly visibly erupt into our material reality.

You`ll want to know the current shape and form of your father`s energy. By walking between the worlds we`ll learn more about a hidden extra dimension of energy which already exists, for all of us, whilst we`re alive in a physical body.

We need to unravel this secret, Sam, since it holds the truth of immortality for everybody. This is going to be quite an experience so if you`re ready, we could start on our journey.

Sam: Okay but I`m a bit of a sceptic and I`m not sure I believe you`ll be able to answer every question I have.

Oh but that is exactly what I am here to do and, before we begin, I want to hear more about the ways in which your father has been in contact with you. I`ll briefly describe some of my own experiences ~ though much more follows later ~ and then we can launch ourselves into the after life world.

Sam`s Story

My father died of cancer so it wasn`t wholly unexpected but when it did happen it was all very fast at the end. He had fallen over and hurt his leg badly so they took him to hospital for an X ray. He had to wait for ages and in fact they kept him in over night.

He`d always been positive and upbeat about his cancer, but when the hospital doctors read his records they filled him with fear and he just gave up and died

I was always very close to my Dad ~ my mother died when I was a child ~ and I`m eighteen now so am away at uni, but managed to be with him when he died.

It was only a week later, before we`d even had the funeral ~ delayed because of the post mortem ~ that I saw him the first* *time. He just stood in the doorway staring at me. I`ve seen him again twice since then but he just stands there, silently.

I do often hear his voice though, it sounds like his voice too, just telling me things and one time he came through and gave me a warning, told me to drive the other way to my normal route, so I did. Afterwards, on the local news, we heard there was a bad accident and I would have been right there, where it happened, if I had gone the normal way.

And things move, my phone disappeared from my bedside table and ended up in his room, and his door was locked on the outside, we never go in there any more. The lights keep going on and off even though I keep changing the bulbs. My phone and computer keep not working without any reason and I don`t smoke but one day Dad`s lighter just appeared on the kitchen table beside me, ***and I don`t know how it got there!***

Another time I left the kitchen with all the stuff on the sides, in a bit of a mess and it was like somebody had come and cleared it all away, pushed it off to the other end in a neat pile with only the bowl for my cereal left out for me, like he used to do, Dad would always put that bowl out for me when I was home.

Please tell me that some of these things have happened to you too. Sometimes I think I`m going mad and I just need some sort of explanation about what is going on here!

My husband died suddenly, unexpectedly over a year ago,at close to midnight, leaving me shattered, disbelieving, shaking.

And yet, just six hours later, just before dawn the next day, he manages to contact me to tell me he is okay.

He does this by projecting an image through the darkness to me. Before I went to bed at about three in the morning, I had noticed a small head and shoulders photograph of Peter, and it is this exact image which now appears.

With one major difference because **this** image is filled with pure white healing light, and through this brilliant white he is telling me that he`s okay, and that his healing has already begun. Next a picture of a tiny white translucent globe comes through almost as though he`s showing me where he is now.

At this stage I have no idea how he can project these images through my energy fields ~ the secret energy force is about to be revealed ~ but several more pictures come through over the next few days. Every one is filled with the same bright white light pure and healing energy.

And every image brings comfort and reassurance.

However, this is just the beginning of a journey of continual appearances, happenings, signs symbols, movements of light and energy which continue to prove he`s still around for me, and capable of answering any question I might throw at him.

I`ll give you the full story at the end of the book, Sam, but just to cite two instances of Peter`s contact: two books and his keyboard suddenly threw themselves down on the floor in front of me one day. They were all on the bookcase, on the landing, and narrowly missed me

I knew he had to be involved in this because material objects don`t just get up and throw themselves without help but what I had to do was to work out why, what message did they have for me? I`ll give you the reasons for all of this later too.

On another occasion Peter knocked over a tall *bubble light* when nobody was anywhere near, and a wash of water flew out and flooded many books and DVDs. This time his message was to slow down instead of pushing myself to finish and publish the book I was working on at the time. Very curiously, the book was called: `A positive **light bubble`.**

Another message was involved with the tumbling over of this lamp which resulted in my being able to attend the funeral of a friend`s husband. Had Peter not pushed over the bubble light I would not even have known this man had died.

Now we have to begin on our journey of exploration through worlds of life, death and beyond. We must now start providing you with all the ample evidence and explanations to prove how we **DO live on after physical death.**

There is so much reassurance which comes from learning and taking note of all these messages which continually come through to us, having been sent by and from our loved ones who have died. They want us to see that this is all proof and evidence of the truth that: **once we leave the physical body, we will continue to exist in a different shape and essence of energy entirely.**

BUT WE DO STILL CONTINUE TO EXIST INDEFINITELY

Your first question was:

Where do we go to when we die? I`ll start giving you the answers ~ relayed to me from the `other` world energy ~ as soon as we`ve heard from Michael and Claire.

Michael`s contact with Claire

This is a family who love the sea. Nineteen year old Claire had gone swimming with her boyfriend but, on one particular day, the tide turned and came back on them. He managed to escape but Claire drowned.

And yet Claire knew it was going to happen. The year before she had asked her father, Michael, what he thought of this `dying lark`, and where he responded that he thought it would be okay, she said she was looking forward to it. They discussed where they would want to be buried and Claire said: `I`d like to die in the sea! `

But she turned to her father and said: `The chances are that you`ll die first because you`re older so will you come back and talk to me? `

`Yes of course I will, and would you do the same for me if, God forbid, it happened the other way around? `

Claire readily agreed that she would, and she has, continually.

At first they could not find her body but the day after she had drowned Michael ~ who was an expert diver ~ went with two friends, feeling he had good knowledge of the area and that he would be the one to find her.

And yet, once he was under the surface, his compass refused to work and from under the water he sensed that he would not be allowed to be the one to find her. She wouldn`t let him find her in case the temptation proved to be too strong to stay down there with her.

Eventually it was one of his friends who found Claire`s body and, when he brought her out of the sea in a plastic bag, Michael was looking down but her voice came through to him: `I`m not down there, I`m up here. `

And suddenly he was aware of her presence around him

at the size of a pea which kept shooting off, whizzing around his shoulder, going out ahead of him into the distance and then bouncing back, and all around him, shouting: `I`m free, I`m free!`

From very shortly afterwards, and across a period of ten weeks, Claire appeared to Michael in various shapes and guises. From being a ball of golden light which seemed to grow in him or he would see her face, or her shape in white, but across every night, between the hours of 4am and 4.30 am, he felt her presence with an energy of love.

`I love you, Dad, ` she would tell him over and over again.

She would talk to him for over half an hour at a time whether he was in a particular place, or on retreat, but she never seemed to appear to other people such as her boyfriend, who was heartbroken to have lost her.

`How come I`m the only one to hear you?` Michael asked.

This was when Claire drew two circles and explained to him that people exist in their own individual separate circles. But when it came to Claire and Michael their circles overlapped and this would always be the way they were able to communicate. All that was needed for them to do so was to step into the overlap.

After the intense ten week period of her appearing Michael had to take a break to regroup his energy, but Claire has continued to appear and talk to him, at different stages, across the last eleven years since she died.

And she has lost none of her sense of humour, still being a `scallywag` as Michael would describe her.

Sometimes she makes faces at him like an impish child and when he asked what her job was in the hereafter she showed him an image of herself doing an Irish jig on the top of tin cans. She described herself as a `tin opener`.

Thoroughly confused by this he asked for an explanation

and she told him it was all to do with love. She said that, in life, people have trouble holding on to the love inside them, that there was nothing or no way to contain the love so that if love could be contained in a tin can then she would help open the tins for them ~ in other words opening their hearts to love. And this was the best way she could describe what was happening from her level of energy.

She has shown him her face as she was when she died, and also as she now is. When he asks for a description of her current shape, or form, she describes herself as: `huge` or in other words covering a large powerful empty space ~ through which everything can `become` or `appear`. She says sthere are little waves at the edges, holding the power to communicate and flowing out with love to everyone.

She helps him in various ways and hit him when he stood on a wood louse telling him not to kill it but simply remove it outside.

On another occasion Claire`s sister was phoning her father and saying she had lost her keys which she desperately needed to take the children to school. Michael went to her house and said he would sit quietly in the lounge and ask Claire to find the keys. He sat down on the settee and Claire shouted out: `They`re underneath your bum, you`re sitting on them! `

Sure enough he was, despite everyone`s disbelief since the keys had definitely not been there before through many previous searches.

Then there was the occasion when Michael was going out diving again and Claire warned him to: `be careful because somebody will get in trouble today`, and he felt he should heed her warning.

The leader of their diving group suggested a morning and afternoon dive and, when they all came back in good order,

Michael thought to himself: `Oh so Claire was wrong then? Yet the dive leader then suggested that they should all undertake a night dive and when they all went out there was, sure enough, one person who panicked and got into difficulties. However Michael was ready and on the alert so he was able to help save the person, all thanks to Claire.

She appears sometimes as a golden ball of light and describes herself to her father now as being `more alive than ever I was since I became`. She tells him about how dying is, in fact, the act of becoming rather than ending, and she has now been `found` instead of being `lost` which is an overworked and irrelevant phrase for when someone has died.

She speaks of herself as consisting of: `atoms in another universe`, and Michael is so reassured that she is completely happy in the vast empty space where she now finds herself.

He is, and always will be, deeply grateful for her ability to continually be in touch with him as this has immeasurably helped his journey through the grief.

Chapter Two

Into a WORLD of ETHER LIGHT

Sam: I always believed there was only one world, this world, so how CAN Dad appear in our world when he`s not here any more? Is there some different world you go to when you die?

Your father is now and always has been created from the same substance, vapour, fluid and medium that fills every part of the universe. Have you ever heard of ether, Sam?

Sam: I`ve heard the word but what is it ~ is it air?

Ether is the high frequency energy which **fills** space and air. The ancients called this other level of energy their `upper air` They believed that when their loved ones died they suddenly found the ability to pass over to the other side into a transparent upper air level of energy. They felt that, from here, they would continue to exist indefinitely, and could be contacted by those still living in the material physical world.

Sam: *So what* **is** *their upper air?*

ETHER, Sam, and this is the same essence and substance from which every one of us was created, originally. Ether flows into every part of the universe and fills all the space in our own bodies. Ether supplies the vital force of life`s existence but also keeps every star and planet in their place in the skies.

If we want to know more about life after death my husband is telling me we have to look into the Ether which is an element like earth, fire, water and air.

Sam: But what does this Ether **do** *and how is Dad connected?*

Remove ether from the picture and there would be no time or

space, in fact nothing at all.

Vitally, Ether is the carrier of light waves without which all of us would die. And as to where you father is now, he continues to exist in his own etheric light body. HE STILL HAS HIS OWN INDIVIDUAL ESSENCE OF ENERGY!

Sam: Is there a whole other world of Ether then?

Yes there is. This world, our tangible world has an outer ring of ether outlining energy which creates the **Ether parallel World.** The invisible world exists just beyond our own and flows along finer, faster, lighter vibrations at the same time interpenetrating and interacting with our world reality.

Sam: What does this Ether World look like?

Whilst invisible to our eyes, this outer world could be visualised as a shining ring of light spinning and spiralling right the way around our visible world, continuously.

In fact NASA has just announced the discovery of a space time vortex which exists around the earth. What they are, in fact, uncovering is the ETHER WORLD.

As we continue in our investigation we need realisation of this outer universal world and to learn of our outer ether body.

Sam: But I don`t get this, why would I need an outer body?

Your ether twin body spins its way around you to supply life force energy, when you`re alive, and this is how you depart when you die. We`ll go into this more later but it is through your own ether twin energy self that your father ~ now an `etheric` ~ is able to contact and connect with you.

Chris was a hiker who spent a great deal of time using his compass when he went out for long hikes with his wife, Patsy. `But Patsy died and I was completely bereft, not knowing what to do with myself without her. Eventually, I started going out for long hikes on my own but very oddly the compass needle would spin around, out of control, each time and I kept getting lost.

It was only as I gradually realised that this was Patsy`s way of contacting me that the compass needle calmed down and began working properly. And I felt so comforted to know she was still around with me, particularly on those hikes. `

Sam: Does the sun have its own ether outline too?

Yes ether energy surrounds and fills everything and provides the missing 99% of space.

Sam: And my father still exists in the Ether parallel world?

Definitely ~ he left his physical body to become wholly ether.

Sam: *Is it through this ether stuff that* **he** *contacts* **me***?*

Yes the messages I`m receiving from the Ether World tell me he no longer needs that physical body to be in touch with you but is using his own supplies of ether energy.

Sam: But I don`t see how this can all work.

Every single movement of energy in this, or the other world, happens through ether energy. The whole universe, Sam, is ether in different states of high fine light vibrational energy.

Mostly, I`m told, ether travels at too high, fast and fine a frequency for us to see except in out of body experiences.

Sam: What **is** *an out of body experience?*

Oh sometimes some kind of trigger sets us off on a journey right out of our physical body. This could be during an operation where the patient finds they lift out of their body entirely and become aware of the energy higher up.

In fact there was a heart surgeon who decided to place obscure images such as an elephant in a tutu and a mouse on a bike out of view above the ceiling lights of his operating theatre. Then, when he had effectively killed people for up to eleven minutes at a time ~ by stopping their hearts ~ as he revived them he asked what they had seen. They all reported back to him that they had been out of their body at a different level, looking down and exactly described the images hidden on the ceiling.

The big difference between death and an OBE is that in being out of the body a silver cord from your ether body is still firmly attached, and you do have the ability to return to physical life.

When we die this silver cord releases its hold on the physical and we move on and away.

Sam: This only gives me part of the picture but what I want to know is what this ether stuff looks like? If its invisible how do I know it`s there?

Ether is almost indescribable unless you think of snow.

Sam: But snow is just a load of white stuff?

Not quite, snow consists of flakes of reflecting white light.
These flakes become a substance when squashed together.
If you boil snow it turns into a vapour then a fluid.
Ether reflects and carries light, is vapour, fluid or substance
Snow swirls subtle energies all around us, as does ether.

Individual snowflakes are more visible once gathered together.

Snow falls, blankets the landscape and fills the atmosphere

Ether layers blanket all creation and fill the atmosphere..

Look through beams of light and sometimes you see tiny fine dust like particles of ether.

Those who have died exist as an individual portion of ether energy, light shines through and spirits become visible. Every action and interaction happens invisibly through ether. But then we can`t see snow till it decides to fall out of the sky.

Snow has a light feel just like ether.

Snow and ether bring white light energy into our reality.

Finding the existence of ether energy transforms our view of life and death. Ether is silent and cold as is snow.

Perhaps snow can help remind us of how our loved ones do still exist, easily and gracefully, in a magical mysterious light filled world which normally we are unable to see?

Sam: Okay so Ether looks like snow and is everywhere yes?

Ether spins spirals and vibrates at fast speeds to carry light and energy into every level and world. Ether supports existence. Your Dad is now wholly made of malleable ether which has depth and a greater density than gold or lead.

Yet ether also has lightness and supranormal powers to make it possible for different dimensions to communicate with each other, by using vibrations. The Ether is the energetic medium for light, radiation, energy and messages to transmit.

As light moves on and into other levels of existence one more soul is admitted to the fold.

All the time energy winks, blinks and flashes in and out of existence, our universe is a continuous hive of activity. Etheric vibrations supply energy for every atom and particle which forms the foundation for the building of life itself.

Sam: That`s a pretty big ask and I`m beginning to see that ether could be necessary. I must admit that I ***have*** *seen flashes of light which could be ether energy. From what your husband is telling you is Dad using ether energy, from where he is now, to make light wink, blink and flash in and out of my world?* Yes and he`s also using ether light vibrations to help you see his energy presence for ether has infinite abilities.

Sam: And it sounds like it has a ghostlike appearance.

Now that is interesting. In fact ether energy is known to concentrate around a specific *ghostlike* subatomic particle and ~ although orthodox science says it can`t happen ~ this is how objects can be moved by and through this invisible substance.

Space and matter are fundamentally identical. They come from the one same vibrating energy source ~ the unifying ether ~ which connects and unifies everything, but they act as different interchangeable phases.

Sir Oliver Lodge said of intrinsic ether: `The total output of a million kilowatt power station for thirty million years exists permanently in every cubic millimetre of space`.

Sam: So how do we move freely in a solid substance which has greater density than lead?

The answer from Sir Oliver was: `Where densities differ sufficiently they can move through each other. ` To sum up on Ether: Ether fills all space, exists beyond physical life and yet supports every part of existence.

When people die they move wholly into the Ether World.

Whilst alive, we have an extra outer ether body and I know you want to learn more about your energy twin but, firstly, ether can also be audible through white noise sounds. These exist as the sound of moving ether energy, sometimes heard when a radio or tv are not tuned in properly, or as Annie found:

Annie`s father Edmund died, and about a week later she was with her sister Julie, alone in the family home.
`At about 3am we thought we ought to go to bed, ` Annie says, `but then the phone rang and when we went to pick it up there was nobody there.
Up to that point we had been reminiscing about how kind and understanding our father had been and we were very surprised that anyone would phone us at that time of the morning, and yet there was only `white noise` on the other end of the line.
We put down the receiver and discussed who it could be.
Then, jokingly, we said that maybe it was Dad?
At this very second the phone rang again as if on cue.
Both of us were feeling a bit spooked at this happening.
I answered the phone again and, once again, there was just `white noise`.
So I replaced the receiver.
My sister and I were seriously spooked by now and then we decided to challenge my Dad. We said: "Okay Dad, if that was you, ring again after the count of 3."
Then we chanted in strict rhythm, one.........two........three.........
Brrrring, brrring, the phone came in right on the beat of 4.
Both of us were so scared we screamed, took the phone off the hook and ran to bed! `

Chapter Three

Your Immortal TWIN SELF

Sam: Okay you speak of a twin self, double body is this like a doppelganger, an avatar or a clone?

Not exactly ~ you, me and everyone else, we all have an outer twin self, a subtle energetic body created entirely of ether energy. This energy body outlines your physical shape and form, extending to one and a half inches out from your skin.

This extra supply of outer energy exists at a higher faster frequency than you normally have with your physical energy. **And this is how you connect and communicate with other dimensions.**

Sam: How can I believe I have this other body if I can`t see it?

Ah but you can see this sunny radiant outline reflecting out from your dense physical body by going outside in the sunshine. With the sun behind you, look down at your own shadow on the ground and it should be possible to see a trace of golden light shimmering around beyond your shadow.

Or imagine this outline as a transparent oval shaped vitamin capsule with your body inside instead of the vitamins.

Your physical body has dense substance and this outer self consists of higher frequency, fast travelling light energy. In art galleries those considered to be Holy have been painted with a halo of light shown round their heads.

Sam: Why only their heads if we all have this radiant outline?
This is because it would have been more visible in those such as Jesus, especially around their head and shoulders. When we die, instead of shutting everything down and becoming a blank

canvas, we **do** leave the physical body behind as an empty shell. However, our consciousness and individual core essence can never be lost. Instead this moves gradually and gracefully out of the physical to become the ether energy body.

Once free, this energy shape ~ now wholly composed of ether ~ can move on and away into the after life realm.

Sam: To become an ether individual?

That`s a good description, Sam. In ancient Egypt they called this subtle outer body the `Ka`. Their Ka, in life or death, was their spirit self and when someone left the physical body behind relatives would still talk, write letters or offer food to their Ka spirit body.

I`m told that we all have this Ka overself and outer consciousness. Your father has merely moved wholly into this high powered spirit body. And since you, too, have an outer Ka body ~ spinning with high light energy right round you ~ this is how he reaches you.

He contacts you through those outer energy fields which spin just like the spin cycle of a spin dryer on the outside of you.

Sam: So this is my second skin or second self?

Yes, you`ve heard of having second sight? Second sight is etheric sight where you can see ether energy shapes. Since ether flows through everything it has these amazing properties.

Your Dad uses ether energy to move light, reflecting it through to you and he can lean on your outline of ether energy to make his presence felt in various ways, to show he is here.

He also moves objects remotely through the ether flow.

Sam: I don`t see how he can do this.

Okay, we`ve discovered the whole universe is filled with

ether and there is an invisible parallel ether world, yes?

Sam: Right but..........

Now see that we`re not the only ones with a light outline.

Every part of nature and creation has its own ether outline.

Every ray, stream or band of light travels in ether levels from the Ether World into our world, highlighting different parts of our reality and shining into our energetic twin body.

When someone comes along and hacks down a tree, or has an operation to remove a limb, the ether outline of the tree or limb remain and exist in the ether level of energy.

In fact some people even report still having pain in their limb once it is removed, but this is the energetic ether feel of their limb not the actual physical arm or leg.

And it is the silver blue light outlining energy round any object which enables that object to be moved.

Sam: Hey that`s clever. So everything has this outer twin?

Yes mountains, stones, trees, all have the same radiating ether light energy which your Dad is using now to communicate with you or to move things around.

This gives us some insight into paranormal and psychic phenomena, or appearances. They happen from a movement of ether energy erupting straight into our visible tangible reality.

Ian McNemara was a mature portrait photographer who hadn`t adapted to digital photography, but he was an expert and he knew what he was doing so that what happened to him, across a period of three weeks after his great friend, Margot, died suddenly should not, technically, have happened at all. There was no obvious cause.

`Every time I went out on a shoot, and this was in high summer when many of my clients liked to have their

photographs taken in the countryside, I found that when the photos were developed there was this strange effect coming through, ` Ian says. `It was almost as though you could see someone`s outline just behind the subject, each time.That extra image or outline always resembled Margot.

Sometimes you can see this strange effect of a kind of white outline around people when on TV, against a dark background, but this was something else entirely because every time it was Margot! I tried changing cameras, films, locations, subjects but it kept on happening on every shoot across those three weeks, and my clients weren`t happy.

But there was nothing I could do as she just kept appearing as though she was trying to give me some kind of message, to tell me she was still around. Despite having to wipe out all my work during those three weeks it was immensely comforting ~ thank you Margot. `

In my own case, six months before my husband died, we took a photo of him on an instamatic camera. Peter had a little dark to grey hair and was clean shaven.

The photograph instantly appeared as the face of a very old wise man with white hair and a white beard as you can see on the cover of this book.

We are creatures of energy with links, filaments, cords or cables of ether reaching out and back through our twin body.

We are all connected to all the energies of our world and also the energies of the unseen unknown world.

This means that we are in constant touch and contact with other levels and dimensions without realising this ability

We come into life through this twin energy shape and continue to exist in this same twin energy form when we die. And within this realisation lies the secret of our immortality.

Our light outlining self, our counterpart, is the blueprint which acts like a map right around us to show all the hundreds of energy interactions happening inside and reflecting in and out and through us all the time. We act like a continual mirror.

Sam: What.... so other people sense what we think and feel?

Oh yes, Sam, but there`s enough material in there to fill a whole other book. * But, right now, we`re concentrating on our sunny Ka outline which reaches out through the aura comprising our emotional, mental and spiritual bodies. Our whole aura can reach from our skin out to forty eight inches

Sam: When Dad appears, is he using his Ka ether body?

He now has all kinds of powers and abilities he never had before whilst he was imprisoned in a physical shell, Sam.

He is now able to mould or reshape his ether energy to resemble the recognisible form he held whilst still alive. Mediums have spiritual sight and can see this shape of energy. Soon I`ll describe how Debbie, the medium, saw my husband ~ through my energy fields ~ at three quite separate times or ages in his life. When your father appeared to you, did he look different from when he was alive?

Sam: No he looked just the same, same age and same clothes only slightly transparent.

This can vary between insubstantial or having substance.

Everything depends on how much energy they are able to project through to this world..

Tom couldn`t believe it. Ruth had died, they had buried her in the ground and he knew she had gone but, yet, she seemed to be standing at the end of the bed, looking like she had years ago when she was younger, wearing that violet dress she loved and she was smiling at him. And yet he could see

the shape of the door behind or through her!
In his ether body, Sam, your Dad affects surrounding ether.
This is how paranormal phenomena happen.
Sam: Have others described this extra body or twin?

Yes I can list some of the descriptions for you:

In Hermetic belief as the:	**Immortal Body**
Through Gnosticism:	**The Radiant Body**
In alchemy	**The Golden Body**
In the mystery schools:	**The Solar Body**
Under Vedanta belief:	The **SuperConductive Body**
In Taoism	**The Diamond Body**
Through Sufism	**The most Sacred Body**
In Ancient Egypt	**Luminous Body or Being (akh)**
Through Sri Aurobindo	**Divine supramental substance**
In Tibetan belief	**The Light Body**

Sam: Hey now I have different ways to see him but I still don`t understand where he gets the power to move energy?

Those who pass over to the other side still have power to manipulate energy, in our world, by using a hidden power force to react with our Ka outlining fields of faster light frequency.

We all have this Ka ether body which protects and connects us with other levels and energy dimensions, and those who have moved on from this mortal life want us to recognise the presence of our own outer twin self.

This is the gift of immortality rediscovered beneath the temple of Jerusalem in the twelfth century. Very coincidentally the Akayshik Hall of Karmic Records is also hidden there.
They contact us by shining through our twinlight outline.

* `A positive light bubble` by the same author

Chapter Four

From music to bananas to motorbikes

Mac was a copyist who used to work with Angus, an orchestrator, who died quite young. Angus and his wife had a friend who was a clairvoyant and out of the blue she phoned through to Mac saying: `You won`t know me but I was a very good friend of Angus and his wife and right now Angus keeps coming through to me. He won`t leave me in peace until I have contacted you and passed on a particular message.

I have had great trouble finding your phone number, but I just know I have to do this and this concerns a piece of music that you are working on now. In the fourth line there is a mistake on the piano part of the music which needs to be changed. `

Mac looks down through the music, firstly looking at a point eight lines down ~ ie in the first system ~ but it seems to be okay. `No this is fine,` he says, wondering what is going on.

But this particular clairvoyant is insistent. `Angus is sure there is something wrong, are you looking four lines down?

`So Mac looks again and now looks at the fourth line which is the second system and in the middle of the line he finds that a crucial mistake has been made. `Oh my God you`re right, there is, and this would have been a disaster if it had been allowed to go through, it would have ruined the whole piece! `

Mac had never believed in life after death but what had just happened to him altered his whole system of belief

So many report ~ following the death of their loved one ~ that: `I just felt his or her presence in the room, near me, or around me somewhere. I know he or she is with me, keeping me company, pointing out something important. `

Jim, a tall though slightly fragile man in his seventies, was so lonely after Mags died, his friends just didn`t know what to say to him any more. They tried to chivvie him along or invite him out but he stayed in all the time not knowing what to do.

He saw her first of all on a Monday and he remembered that particularly because it was after Sunday which was always the longest day of the week for him. He never even seemed to have any phone calls on a Sunday.

When his friends asked for descriptions of how she looked, he couldn`t say exactly. ` I could see her face but not all of her face, rather the nose and the mouth and then the eyes as separate items rather than all together. But as I saw her nose I felt that she pressed on my nose, I could feel a pressure as though she was touching my nose, mouth and then my eyes.

And then whilst I couldn`t hear her voice either in my head or out loud I just knew that she was urging me to do something. She wanted me to find a way to stop being so lonely, but this didn`t have to involve going out and being with other people because I just wasn`t ready to do that at this stage. There was a pen on the desk in front of me and I felt rather than saw it move, it moved nearer to my hand. She wanted me to pick it up and do something with it, to start writing.

"You want me to write my own diary or a book about how I can see and feel you here with me today?" I asked her and I could swear that pen grew warm in my hand, there was definitely a change in temperature.

I`ve been doing this ever since. She often appears in the same way and its helping me so much to get through my grief by putting it all down, sometimes as a diary and sometimes in letters addressed to her directly to tell her what is going on in my life. More is going on, I get out more and knowing she`s around and writing my feelings down gives me confidence. `

Janet`s husband had always been very lively with a great sense of humour and he had always loved bananas although she didn`t, but after he died she kept buying them in case

the children wanted to eat them. One day she was downstairs ~ the kitchen was on the top floor ~ when she heard a thud, and since she had both cats with her in the room she knew it wasn`t them.

But on going up she found that the bunch of bananas had somehow been launched out of the fruit bowl and were now lying on the floor. This was Sandy`s way of telling her that not only was he still around but that he ~ who had loved his food ~ was getting hungry.

Janet`s second husband was Mike and one of his proud boasts was that when he was training at Kings hospital he and another case officer had swopped duties and roles. Though he was not in the obstetric field of work, one day when a black lady suddenly went in to labour Mike stepped forward and helped to deliver the baby. He was always very proud of this achievement.

Just after Mike died ~ again curiously in Kings ~ Janet went out for a smoke. When she came back she found a black lady had gone into labour, amidst much running of feet and urgent calls from the staff, and she was right outside the door of the room where Mike`s now silent body still lay.

Rachel had a friend whose partner died and they all got together to try to reconnect with him. She asked for a sign to show he was around and a ladybird popped in to her head and she couldnt think why. Afterwards it was one of their birthdays and someone came up with a present right on top of which was a chocolate ladybird ~ definitely sent from beyond!

Then there is Keri who went on a holiday with friends to Barcelona. One night and for no reason whatsoever she just passed right out and as she was going she was aware of a spiralling shining light, then nothing. Obviously her

friends fussed about her, after she came round, but she had hardly had anything to drink, and her health was fine. She was not given to passing out, so there was no obvious reason for what happened.

She thought nothing more about it on her holiday and yet when she came back she learned that a good friend of her`s had died, on exactly the day and time when she passed out.

His funeral had already taken place so she never really had a chance to say goodbye.

After this time she went on a course about becoming a medium and at the end of the course they all underwent a meditation process. During this meditation she saw that same sense of a white spiralling light spinning off into the distance. Following the meditation the person who was taking the course practised some of her mediumistic abilities and passed on messages to the students. One of these messages was from a biker who had recently died and wished to say goodbye to his friend in the class. He said that previously he had only been able to say goodbye by sending through a spiralling shining essence of white light.

Keri`s friend ~ who died on the night she passed out ~ had been a biker!

Children talk to people who are invisible to their parents, all the time, and this is particularly heightened when a loved one or member of the family has died although the parents might not even know of the death, at the time.

Tod was only three years old and suddenly became very busy and involved with talking to someone his parents couldn`t see. They thought this must be some kind of imaginary friend so took little notice. It was the day after this started that Becky went to answer the phone only to be told that her beloved Uncle Henry had died in a car accident. He had always been her favourite uncle, but he was living in Canada and they hadn`t been over to see him since Tod was born because they couldn`t afford to go.

Becky was in floods of tears on hearing the news and Neil came up and asked her whatever was the matter? But at this stage, before she could say anything, Tod spoke up and told his father, `Mummy`s crying about Great Uncle Henry, but he says not to cry, he`s very happy and he`s sending some money through to her soon for her to visit his country, where he lived.`

Becky was not only shocked at his awareness but to her knowledge she had never described her Uncle Henry as great Uncle Henry to Tod, how could he have known the relationship between his great uncle and himself when he was only three years old? She realised that this must have been who he was talking to the day before, exactly when Uncle Henry had died.

And two weeks later she was notified that she would receive some money from his estate. His special request was that she should travel and take her husband and young son to Canada, to see the rest of the family.

Einstein said: ` the field is the sole governing agency of matter. Fields of energy dictate the behaviour of everything from subatomic particles to massive planets. `

We **all** and every one pass over from life in a physical body and move into our ether light body as our spiritual self.

We all assume this shining white light body so, in effect, all of us resurrect although we don`t appear to all have the ability to be seen visibly in this shape by those left behind.

Jesus wanted us to know that we all held this ability but we have long been too blocked and afraid to allow ourselves the chance to see how and who we become after the death of our physical body. In fact we are generally all afraid of death despite this simply being the death of the ego followed by a state of enlightenment, taking us to a far better place than here.

Chapter Five

A Hidden FORCE OF ENERGY

Sam: Okay so now Dad is in this Ether World but where does he get the power to move things in our world?

An incredible vital energy force exists in our universe.

Whilst hidden this force exists and flows everywhere.

And, under certain conditions, the effects of this force become visible...... light radiates out from inanimate objects!

If you want to know more about how the invisible becomes visible we need to go back to the eighteenth century.

Sam: But why have we never heard about this hidden force?

You mean apart from Star Wars? Seriously, this vital force was discovered, by accident in the first place, by a certain Baron in 1785. He had been undertaking experiments on sensitive people with a habit of sleepwalking, trying to find out why they kept ending up at the top of buildings at night.

What he began to find was the existence of a force of energy ~ possibly connected with the moon ~ drawing them up there.

Sam: Who was this man then?

Carl Von Reichenbach, a metallurgist, naturalist and philosopher, also studying life related energies........

Sam: An original psychic investigator?

Yes, possibly, but he never expected to make such a profound discovery. He began to realise that this impulse to walk in your sleep comes from cosmic light rays, and this forced him to undertake experiments in his castle in Austria.

Sam: Now it sounds like Dracula!

One similarity is the Baron`s work must happen in the dark! He starts conducting moonlight beams through wire braids.

Next he asks his sensitive subjects to hold these braids and tell him whether they feel heat or cold? He`s very surprised to find heat comes from moonlight, and cold from sunlight. Now all kinds of unexpected things start happening.

Sam: What kind of things? Don`t keep me in suspense.

Well now these sensitive people not only feel temperature changes but they`re aware of weird unearthly light flashes from nowhere, bursting through the darkness. The Baron can`t see this so has to keep asking questions. They describe seeing this flame-like radiance which glows around certain objects.

Carl realises some kind of energy force has to be involved, not light, but able to be conducted as visible light fields ~ like the aureola borealis ~ to create great displays of light.

Flashing, intertwining light dances through darkness in shapes of green and purple cosmic light fire and he finds this force is neither electrical nor magnetic, that it can be stored and reflected from mirrors, but that it breaks all scientific laws.

He needs an explanation and asks other prominent scientists around him. Yet they retreat and run scared from something which seems so inexplicable. They say: LEAVE IT ALONE.

This Baron, however, feels this is a life changing discovery. Metal objects are able to radiate flames of light because of this force. Luminous light appears in streams from out of the invisible ether, combusting spontaneously in streaks and flares.

He begins to ask himself: `**could this force come from another dimension entirely to be creating this twilight zone phosphorescent effect?`**

Sam: `So does this force have a name? `

The Baron calls this `Odic fluid` or the `Odin or Od` force.

Sam: `This could have been named for the Norse God to show power but Od is not a good word these days.

I agree. I`ve looked up Odin`s relations to find he had a grandson called: `Magni` so this could be the: `Magni Force?

Sam: I like that, tell me more about the Magni Force.

Our Baron now knows he`s made a spectacular discovery of a force of energy which comes from some hidden unknown dimension, can travel, appear and disappear at whim and almost seems to be manipulated by unknown hands.

Sam: The same force which causes paranormal phenomena?

Definitely ~ when paranormal phenomena happen, charges of energy cause spontaneous eruptions in our reality.

All these strange happenings prove the existence of a hidden dimension or world of energy where impossible things happen.

Now the Baron goes from strength to strength, uses crystals to scatter light and his subjects see rainboid auric effects round certain objects which pulse out light rays from a hidden source.

Gradually Carl, too, sees the effects of sharp light rays quivering with energy. **In modern day Kirlian aura photography light is seen as spiky lines in different colours.**

This energy force moves from place to place with an inherent ability to flow more strongly in some places than others

Sam: Like where for instance?

Graveyards, in the darkness, near newly dug graves where forces of magnetism from the earth are most extreme!

Th*is energy force* travels along light beams, through the Ether, so now the Baron uses sun, even starlight in his investigations. Each time inactive molecules suddenly find the new power source from inside to erupt into life.

Sam: So how can those who have died use the Magni Force?

They act as receiving and conducting energies to transmit light beams through the ether and this has an effect in our world. And Carl now constructs giant receiving plates on the castle roof to transmit powerful light beams. He achieves spectacular results but always has to insist on silence.

Sam: Why would his subjects have to be silent?

Their talking causes movements of air which, in turn, affect the shape of what is about to become visible.

Sam: What else do they see?

Vibrant flames climbing, flaring, dazzling from nowhere and what they are seeing is the radiant light field which exists everywhere, around everybody and everything. The proof is being given to them of how **paranormal psychic phenomena are projected from remote places ~ from somewhere else!**

The Baron`s metal plates on the roof are relaying and passing on this hidden energy force, via light beams, in the same way as those on the other side of life are able to do. Next he sets up a battery of different types of plates to try to change the colour of the flames.

And his researchers now describe dazzling blue and green flames appearing as copper plates are used. They see flames of pure white when gold and silver plates are tried. Grey blue flames appear by using lead and red white flames from zinc.

When moonlight saturates the plates his sensitives see different shaped flames, more tufted, flaring light outwards just like a halo instead of climbing straight upwards.

T*his kind of flaring light effect has been reported in present day psychic phenomena where light suddenly flares and radiates outwards from objects.*

*F*lames can reach ten or more inches from the wires but the Baron has to know where this mysterious light is coming from?

Sam: He does know it`s not coming from our world?

Yes Carl sees this more as an etheric echo of the force of light which exists around every one of us as an extra layer.

And now his subjects feel cold spreading through their bodies when they hold the wires.

Sam: Hey I have this cold feeling when my Dad is around.

Yet more proof that the energy comes from another outer world. The energy of the Ether has no temperature so the more otherworld ether is around the colder it will be.

H*ere is this Baron discovering an energy which spontaneously creates strange lights from ordinary everyday objects ~ like piles of paper, leather and other natural materials ~ but the scientific world just ignores his findings.*

For the rest of us, however, this is the proof we need of the existence of another level world energy having access to this extraordinary energy force normally hidden and kept secret from our reality.

Sam: Does anything else happen for the Baron?

Oh yes the Baron and his helpers do see other things. They conduct the energy force along electrically insulated silks or cotton threads, through long glass rods or wooden dowels and begin to see how the vital force can move objects.

At first nobody believes what they`re seeing but the Baron explains that the radiant energy currents are being produced inside objects ~ previously saturated with light ~ and when the light reaches a peak.......... objects are bound to move.

Flames leap across gaps and barriers that should, logically, have been resistant. Now there is no holding this power!

There is a glowing light ~ several feet in depth ~ working its way right across the ceiling and, as everyone looks up, they see actual faces in amongst the luminous light shapes.

Now, their own bodies and in fact the whole room becomes freezing cold. Gradually, disbelievingly, they watch the light which begins to reflect from the tips of their own fingers with a weird radiance.

All around them luminous radiant light currents glow with natural phosphorescence.

Sam: You mention faces and shapes, what kind of shapes?

The faces can never quite be identified because they`re very faint but brighter shapes such as cones, rings or balls of light appear, these days we call these light balls ~ orbs ~ and sometimes they seem to bounce off into the distance.

These are very similar to the patterns of light many have reported seeing when a loved one has died.

These eighteenth century investigators make crystals stream with magnified fire and lines of brilliant white when they have been energised by rays of sun or moonlight. Flames shudder and divide when someone blows on them gently. Over and again they prove that this forceful energy charge is coming from another realm and level of energy entirely.

In the human body this force concentrates in the solar plexus and sensitive places like foreheads, lips, face, fingertips, feet and toes. This explains those instances where people have reported being touched on the head or face when someone has died. Or otherwise felt like a breath of air to prove they`re here. **Messages, signs, signals and material phenomena happen in our realm because of the Magni force energy charge.**

Sam: Why can this unearthly ghostly light only be seen in the darkness and is this something to do with ghosts?

When we look into total darkness we pull in abilities from the etheric level of our energy, beyond our five sense reality.

Those in the Ether World are able to make objects move, ether shapes appear, lights flash, sounds echo, voices resonate as they manipulate ether light by using the Magni force energy.

After the Baron`s time it was confirmed the vital *ether* body emanates rays known as Odic fluid. After death of the physical the ether self has greatly increased power to generate these rays THIS BRINGS EVIDENCE OF AFTER LIFE EXISTENCE.

Ether carries vital Odic or magni force power from the sun which vitalizes our twin self energy. This gives our outlining Ka body a similar power to that of those in the Ether World.

Just as a point of very curious interest, Baron Carl Von Reichenbach`s castle was in a place in Bavaria called Regensberg, and on July 18th 2001 there were reports of circles of light ~ with light crosses inside them ~ appearing on various buildings all over the area. However, nobody could ever explain quite why or how this could happen!

Chapter Six

Unearthly *Messages from machines*

Margot`s husband had died in January. She was so lonely and couldn`t bear the silence in the house. She needed the reassurance of having voices around her. `I kept the radio on almost continuously, ` the kindly lady in her late sixties told me `Sometimes I liked to listen to the music programmes, and at other times I would listen to the discussions. I just wanted to feel involved which radio 4 could give me.

On one particular day I was listening to Classic FM and enjoying a piece of music by Bach while I was clearing up the kitchen. The radio was in the sitting room, not close to where I was, but gradually I found I could hear this voice which was cutting in right through the middle of the piece of music.

"Oh these people, why do they interrupt like that just when I`m enjoying the music, too?" I said this out loud and felt really annnoyed as I went into the sitting room to see what was going on. It must be something important to keep interrupting.

But by the time I reached the radio, there was no sound of a voice at all, just Bach`s music playing again so I went back into the kitchen. And just as I was going through the door I heard the voice again, a man`s voice cutting out the music.

I was overwhelmed to find that I recognised that voice! It was Bill`s voice, definitely Bill, but I had to keep telling myself that he was dead, he died of prostate cancer eight weeks before, poor Bill he had been so sick ~ it couldn`t be him!

I ran to put myself right beside the radio to hear the words but, as I approached the radio, the music came back and the voice faded. I couldn`t believe any of this.

I kept on going back in towards the kitchen and each time I went through the doorway, the voice started again. Every time I hurried back to the radio and it stopped.

This pattern continued right the way through the piece of music by Bach, which Bill had known was one of my favourites, but as the music ended the presenter came back on and the programme carried on normally. He`d gone by this time though

And I just knew it was Bill. My hearing isn`t very good and there had been a slight crackling, but there was always an edge and a depth to his voice which was quite unique. The only words I managed to catch were: `well, and here. `

I felt very frustrated that I couldn`t get the whole message but with time I began to realise that was all I needed to know, just that he was still around somewhere and he was well. `

John is an architect, in his forties, and his partner, Christine, had died in a skiing accident. `I was distraught, I just didn`t know what to do with myself, ` he said. `All my energy had gone, I couldn`t work or read a book, not even a newspaper.

And I hadn`t bothered to change the answerphone message because I liked hearing the sound of Christine`s voice. I had been out shopping just for basic food on one particular day, a Wednesday, and I felt slightly better, though only very slightly, when I met up with an old friend who wasn`t overwhelmingly sympathetic like everyone else was being. Somehow all this sympathy was drowning me, dragging me down into self pity.

My friend, Andrew, made me feel a bit better about myself, and my whole future, and I came back to the flat determined to get going and start cleaning the place up.

I pressed the answerphone button to see if there were any messages, not because I wanted to hear them, but just as something to do. Then I heard this very faint sound, a lot of static or white noise but it was Christine, it was her voice!

This wasn`t her recorded message but this was something

else. I had to stand stock still with this growing, mounting feeling of excitement mixed with disbelief and I could hardly make out the words even though I played the voice over and over again.

`You must..........., ` I couldn`t hear the next word at all.......`and I know...............` again the words wouldn`t come through, `but I...........love.............` that was all I could make out clearly but this was more than enough for me.

I could feel from her words that Christine was reminding me that I must go on, that I would be okay and that wherever she was now, she could still love me from there. I felt so grateful! `

Carla was living in Sheffield and, unfortunately, became involved in some gang violence and then there was a tragic accident where she received a blow to her head which was fatal. She was only twenty years old. For both her parents this was an event almost impossible to come to terms with. Her father was a Christian who nevertheless believed that death was the end of everything.

Her mother had always swayed in her beliefs but by this stage felt she no longer believed in anything at all since life had seen fit to take away her beloved daughter.

Yet six months after Carla died, Val answered the phone and it was the operator asking her if she would take a reversed charge call, and then she gave the number the call was coming from, a familiar number to Val since this was Carla`s number.

Val cried out, began to go dizzy and couldn`t answer and her husband, Mark, who was by now standing beside her, took the phone from her whilst trying to hold her up with the other hand. The same message was repeated to him. `Yes of course we`ll take the call, ` he replied hardly knowing what he was saying as the same phone number was given to him by the operator, and some voice inside his head tried to tell him it might be his daughter`s landlord, somebody now using the line.

What he heard once the operator had connected him to the caller`s line was static, whooshing waves of noise and a single word which changed his life and his beliefs from that moment onwards. The only word he could hear through the background noise was: `me` and he was sure it was Carla`s voice that gave that word to him.

But she also gave to him the belief that life does go on and that she is still around.

They checked with the phone company afterwards but it was confirmed, by the operator, that nobody had made a call to their number over the last twenty four hours.

Barbara had thrown her husband`s mobile away after he died. `I was so upset that I didn`t want anything to do with it, and I didn`t want anyone else to use it so I buried it in the garden. On one particular day my own mobile rang and the caller display showed his number, Jon`s number, as though his phone was calling mine!

I quickly pressed the answer button on my phone and of course there was nobody there.

After this I went out to the garden and dug down imagining all kinds of scenarios where a dog could have dug up the phone, and somebody else could be using it, but the phone was still there, covered in earth, exactly where I had left it. `

Dee`s husband Mike died but she was to experience all kinds of happenings connected with machines especially at the time when she decided to throw a seventieth birthday party for him, six months after the date of his death. Mike did not want the party.

As she was trying to make all the arrangements Dee used Mike`s computer and, although she had never had any problem with this machine before, she found two separate CDs which she placed in the computer and the whole thing started whirring and grinding.

So she tried again with a CD of the music she had chosen to use for a slide show for the party. Immediately everything went blank. She called her computer guru friend to come over and he said that the hard drive had just suddenly gone which, if that were the only thing to happen, would have been acceptable. But, added to all the other events surrounding this party weekend, Dee, the sceptic, began to realise that something strange was going on.

She tried to play the CDs on a different machine but they kept shuddering and refusing to play the music properly.

At the actual party, the guy who was playing the DVDs was a friend of Mike`s from his schooldays, and he found that everything he tried to show went completely blank.

Dee had given up her bedroom for old friends to stay at the weekend. When they went out she went to leave extra pillows in the room. She found the alarm clock radio was blinking on the time of 12 o clock ~ midnight ~ and she couldn`t understand why anyone would set the alarm for that time. There was no power cut that night but the cooker

light started flashing and security lights began to buzz.
The jacuzzi suddenly, completely and for no apparent reason emptied itself of water. Then a friend went outside and said it was raining but what was actually happening was the jacuzzi was spouting water out all around even though it was, by this time, completely empty. Dee just couldn`t understand how this could be happening and has had no problem with it since.

A friend, Kelly, was supposed to drive back on the Sunday but her car wouldn`t start so she stayed on in Mike and Dee`s room and became ill overnight. She had the distinct feeling she shouldn`t have been in that room.

All in all every event, added together, seems to point to the fact Mike was trying to stop that party from happening

I myself attended the party and noticed a strange event on my own computer when I received the invitation. My computer immediately flagged up that there was a virus connected with the invitation although the computer had trapped and dealt with it by then.

I completely forgot about this and then, two weeks later, when Dee sent through copies of the photos of the party, the same thing happened again.

It was a month later that I mentioned this to Dee and she said nobody else had had any problem at all. Could it be that Mike was trying to get through to me, by this stage, to accentuate that he did not want that party to happen? Or was he trying to provide another story for this book to help me show how after life phenomena can and do happen?

People have felt, heard and even smelt their loved ones around after they have died, but machines do provide a very convenient way for those in the Ether World to contact us.

Chapter Seven

How do THEY contact US?

Sam: Are they still nearby in their parallel ether world?

Yes, absolutely, our whole universe acts as one unified field of energy. Ether vibrations may be higher, faster and finer than those we use normally, but they do still exist everywhere.

Your father`s ether self now vibrates energy at super high frequencies, but he can reach you through your energy body.

S*am: What individual response could my Dad still have?*

He may no longer have a physical body but your Dad does still have a type of energy. All energy has a will, a force of action and an intention to make something happen. He **wills** his share of ether energy to affect and move light vibrations.

Light uses resonance to increase the frequency.

Sam: Help I don`t understand frequency or resonance.

The frequency is the number of times a vibration repeats itself. Resonance is energy vibrating, reverberating, echoing or ringing in sympathy with a neighbouring source.

As an example of resonance think of a very high pitched voice making a glass shatter. This happens because of the frequency or the number of times the energy vibrates to reach a high pitch. With the glass this is sound resonance or echoing.

Once someone dies, they consist only of ether energy with the power to focus fast vibrating light rays where they choose.

Annie was staying temporarily with her mother after her father`s death. When she went into a particular room she heard this strange noise coming from her sponge bag.

Her mother came to see where the noise was coming from? And when Annie looked inside the sponge bag she found her Phillips ladyshave had decided to keep making this buzzing noise. Somehow, the switch seemed to have slid along and turned itself on. Annie quickly turned it off but then it happened again!

`I know your father was a bit of a practical joker but he doesn`t need to keep doing that to prove he`s still here, ` her mother said. However, the noise refused to stop until they physically had to remove the batteries.

Sam: Do spirits always move energy as they intend to do?

No, definitely not, sometimes they get it all wrong. The connection between their world and our world can be very fragile, and needs practice to master. All kinds of disruption happen in our world energy as lights, electricity and machines switch off and on as those of the other world learn how to handle this elusive energy in the way they plan to do.

The finer more delicate frequency does need practice.

Pat wasn`t sure where she was after her father had died. She had been living with him, in his house, and suddenly it was a very lonely place to be. ` But then, ` she says, `I began to hear the click of the kettle as though it was being switched on and off when I was alone in the house.

The trouble was this kept happening when there was hardly any water in it, my kettles kept burning out. Obviously I filled the kettle up with as much water as possible, each time I used it, but it almost seemed as though the water was draining away somewhere. Over and again each kettle ended up by being empty and, when empty, switched itself on.

I went to visit a medium two months after Dad died and the medium quickly came out with a message, saying it was

Dad, and that he wanted to apologise.

`Apologise ~ why would he want to apologise, he couldn`t help dying from cancer. We do miss him badly but there`s nothing for this good man to apologise for. `

But the medium shook her head and said, `No, he definitely wants to apologise to you about the kettle. `

`The kettle but..........` and then it hit me. `Of course, when alive he was always letting the kettle boil dry.

`Yes, it was his way of reaching through to you, he wanted you to know he is still here and so he used the kettle hoping you would remember what he used to do. But, of course, you obviously didn`t at first, though you do now. ` Once the medium explained we managed to have a good laugh about it all and I felt so reassured, even more than with the messages the medium gave me. `

Sam: So this Ether World is accessible to us?

Yes each one of us has an extra dimension of energy through which to change our own reality. This is what psychics and healers use ~ this sixth sense or etheric second sight.

Ether and the magni force hold the key to the whole secret of existence, after death, and it is intention which causes the seemingly inexplicable phenomena to happen all around us.

Sam: From the Ether World they move light and ether?

They can put pressure on and through ether substance.

Pressures of ether are greater than the normal pressure which the atmosphere exerts on us, but are usually undetectable. Sometimes, if we`re very lucky, we can feel this exchange of energy from the after life as a touch on the face or head or where there seems to be a gentle breath of air moving past.

Robin felt a warm sense of energy wrapped right around her just one day after her husband died.

`It was as though he was still there, he hadn`t gone at all, I felt a reassuring sense of his presence giving an energy hug. The Ether is the means and medium for the transportation of energy through the universe.

Those who have died can use the density of ether to assume recognised shape and form to appear in our world.

With the invisible world existing as another realm of energy we all need to know that **we, too,** are part of this energy, and that we **do** continue to exist after physical death.

Yogic masters confirm that there **is** a source of energy in the human body other than the ones we currently know or have awareness of existing.

Sir Oliver Lodge, the scientist was the first person to ever send a radio message and he stated that he had been in touch with the minds of certain people who have parted from their bodies. `How can a mind get in touch with us when it has no body? ` He asked. `It must borrow some material from spirits and spirits must have substantial bodies not made up of matter but as, I think, the ether`.

Those who pass into the other parallel world use the malleable substance of the Ether to put pressure through our atmosphere, or else use fast vibrations of light to produce paranormal or psychic phenomena to try to gain our attention THEY WANT US TO KNOW THEY STILL EXIST.

There are two levels of reality: our physical material world where the atoms of this world are known to be 99 percent space ~ ie ether energy ~ and the etheric realm.

Rudolf Steiner was an Austrian philosopher and esotericist who lived from 1861 – 1925 and he worked through all kinds of theories about the etheric body, Sam. He believes that every memory we ever have impresses itself on our ether body.

He also relates how there is an imprint on the universal ether. He says that the etheric body is the subconscious, split into three chambers which are spirit, etheric and personality.

Sam: Okay, I thought our subconscious minds stored all our memories. Now Steiner says our etheric energy body consists of spirit, ego and personality, so where are our memories?

I`m told that our individual memories ~ or the after image of everything about us ~ is stored not only in our individual ether body, but also the memory imprint of every single interaction, word, thought and movement of energy we ever use. This includes all the karmic implications and is held in the vast store which is the Akayshic Hall of Records, in the deep ether levels.

Sam: I`ve heard of this but where on the earth is it?

Word has always been out that this Hall of Records lies somewhere beneath Egypt`s Sphinx but Peter tells me differently. He tells me that the Akayshic Hall of Records lies buried deep beneath Jerusalem.

Sam: Oh but this could explain so much. All of this warring and battle between different religions for ownership of various parts of Jerusalem, and wasn`t this where not only Jesus was but from where Mohammed ascended to heaven?

Yes so many events have happened up above this energetically vibrating hall of recorded karmic information lying beneath the city of Jerusalem.

Not only Herod but vitally King Solomon chose Jerusalem as the site of his own wisdom temple.

The Ark of the Covenant was said to lie in the Holy of Holies within that temple. The Knights Templars found their wisdom treasure in Jerusalem, in the stables below the one time temple.

Their secret discovery involved a cloak of light or immortal ether body. Some say they found the head of John the Baptist but this was, instead, the etheric light double of the Baptist`s head.. Abraham, Elijah and David also revered the city.

It is through the universal memories stored in the Hall of Records, in Jerusalem, that ether individuals can assume the shape or form of any previous memory.

In ancient Atlantis the people communicated with each other through their light energy field, whilst still alive in a physical body. But they lost this gift because they were tampering with the DNA, trying to combine animals with humans.

Following the death of Jesus, the disciples were said to have received the Holy Spirit which gave them the ability to be aware of their own outer light energy field, to shine and radiate spirit light out to everybody.

When we`re alive our ether light inside shows our spirit energy, and this spirit light continues indefinitely after we die.

We are all light filled spirit energy and right now we`re having a physical experience. However, we never lose contact with our energetic twin or body double.

This is just the beginning, Sam, we still have to investigate worlds of light, power and energy to gain the full picture of after life contact. Also, on the way, we`re going to find out how it feels to die, and what lies beyond the supposed veil of death from those who have already arrived in the Ether World.

We need to ***feel*** the energy from their world.

Darren`s mother was a smoker and a while after she died he was living on his own, had given up smoking and had no cigarettes in the house, but when he came down to the kitchen one day, he could smell cigarette smoke

And there, on the table was a lit roll up cigarette, balanced in the ashtray with the smoke rising to the ceiling.

His mother died when his son was three weeks old ~ she waited to go till the baby arrived~ and shortly after she had died she moved the cover off the cot and put it on the settee to prove she was still around and watching over the baby.

Chapter Eight

The TWIN BODY at DEATH

Sam: How do we swop to be just an ether body when we die?

As someone goes through the process of death, the whole feel of their subtle energy levels ~ normally quietly vibrating away in the background ~ change dramatically. The life force is preparing to leave from every level of physical existence.

Each of the seven levels of the aura connects to the ether body through fast spinning energy windows, known as `chakras`. These energetic windows vibrate energy out FROM our twin body TO our physical body and BACK AGAIN.

Roughly two days before a person dies, dramatic changes begin to be felt through the ether energy body. This is bound to affect the person though they won`t know what is happening.

Their whole energetic outline gradually expands as greater amounts of light energy, from the Ether, flow into their energy body to help prepare them for what is to come.

Now an ethereal glow surrounds the whole body which even the greatest of psychics can seldom see. The person experiencing these energy changes could be feeling slightly uplifted, and have more energy, but this is only be temporary.

All the time their subtle intangible energies are busy working away to convert, rework and prepare the person for the change which, by now, has to happen.

If you ask anyone who has nursed people approaching death they`ll tell you how, quite often, patients suddenly rally about two days before they die, for no apparent reason.

The patient may want to eat more because their subtle energy is increasing as the inner energy contours expand. Across these next two days, leading up to the moment of death, the person experiencing all these changing inner feelings could be feeling light-headed, or they might even `see` things which somehow don`t quite make sense. This is all to do with a temporary ~ and to them totally new ~ brief ability to have glimpses into another world or level of energy entirely.

This level or world is subtle and beyond their normal range of vision, but they could be aware of transparent shapes moving just slightly beyond their normal range of vision.

About an hour before he died my husband suddenly had what can only be described as a far away look in his eyes, as though he was already half somewhere else and no longer with me, and before his eyes had opened this particular time there was a translucent effect through his eyelids as though he could see out and beyond the shutters which eyelids normally provide to the world around.

Now we`re getting near to the end and the whole illuminated energy field must change dramatically because this will be how the spirit essence of their soul is going to leave the physical body. In other words the way the person will die to become wholly their ether spirit self.

The echoing energy gradually alters, colours change, lessen in intensity, and the whole outline shrinks inwards in a final act of protection for the physical body.

As the brain closes down and ceases to function, the surrounding field of electromagnetic energy dissolves, echoing through subtle shades of grey. This is an effect from all those negative emotions which have been ~ and probably still are ~ around in a person`s energy fields if they have not thus far been able to release them.

I, personally, had absolutely no idea that my husband was dying. He had felt a little uncomfortable and unwell, complained of various pains and feeling nauseous and grew very hot and clammy but nothing was extreme enough for me to feel I needed to call for help.

However, for some reason that I am still completely unable to explain I was willing him, in my mind though not out loud, to forgive his sister for all the upset and great problems ~ involved with a family inheritance ~ he felt she had caused him across the two previous years. I even went to the extreme of finding and placing under his pillow a photograph of his sister. All I can hope is that, on some level, he did hear me and did manage to forgive her completely before he died thus releasing the overwhelming anger that had built up inside him which had all been aimed in her direction and, hopefully, clearing some of that grey negative energy still existing in his energy field.

As death approaches those who follow various religions sometimes feel a need to call for the priest to shrive them to confess their sins, while they still have time. They hope this will lessen the burden of their life review, or when they are expecting to have to face up to their Maker.

Sam: Is this involved with karma, at this stage? Do we all have our karmic obligations and things to work through in life? If we fail to learn from the experience similar things have to keep happening in our next life ~is that how it works?

This is a whole different subject that we`ll be looking at later, Sam, but in effect there is, around this time in the journey, a sense of inner knowing about the karmic load and obligations which each person has set up for themselves from their current life. If these are not released before they die, then that negative karma will be carried on to provide the experiences of another life, and returned to them in various ways, depending on how they have just lived their life.

The life review has to happen, and we will look into this, but there is often an inner feel of urgent need to confess negative `sins` to a priest before death takes place.

But what is happening now in the process is that the whole

energy outline has to suddenly expand rapidly, reaching out through layers of radiancy way out beyond the body, preparing the subtle energy body to take the journey home to the other etheric world.

Now subtle pale blue filters through infinite silver creating white sparks and bubbles of light and, at this point, as all these subtle changes take place, the sensation may be of discomfort and a sense of disorientation for the person who is dying. Yet at the same time they are filled with an unexpected and profound sense of love which wells up to help them overcome any feelings of pain from the physical body.............and this is already beginning to fade.

For them time seems to stop ~ as it does for others involved in the whole area surrounding their death ~ and their energy field around their body weakens to an etherial glow which gradually dilutes.

The vibrating energy outline which has bound the spirit ~ and in turn animated the physical body ~ is now ready to depart from physical matter, to release the silver cord which has bound it in and to life, and lift up through the different levels.

The true light essence of the person disengages from the life force energy of this particular incarnation. Now this energy self moves to a different higher dimensional feel of light energy, in the etheric world, as the highest of all the energy centres envelops the others below. This appears like a veil to provide a flimsy light covering for the forthcoming journey.

The subtle body chooses to exit from physical life by means of the one particular level which, in life, has been most connected with the soul`s intended growth.

In my husband`s case he departed through the solar plexus chakra since it was his emotional level through which he had the greatest learning to do within his lifetime and since you have told me, Sam, that your father could never handle or

face his emotions it was probably the same for him too.

Having been released from the holding cord, the whole energy outline rises as a glowing ball of light and hovers, for a short while, a few feet above the physical body, shining with soft blue light as the life force becomes the **light** force. If we could see this little echoing light what we would see would be the shining brilliant radiating force of a star, glowing luminously.

Sam: I wouldn`t mind being a star but somebody said to me that our energy can`t continue after we die because there wouldn`t be room enough, in the universe, for all the souls to continue to exist. Yet there are billions of galaxies with trillions of stars in the universe so that if everyone became a star there would always be plenty of room. And, of course, stars die and are renewed over time, so there will be even more room.

Now though I want to ask you, I`ve heard somewhere something about a doorway between worlds which stays open for forty hours after someone has died ~ is this true?

In some areas there is a belief that the doorway between the worlds stays open for forty hours after death. This is so that they can sometimes be helped, by those left behind, to pass more easily through to the time of meeting up with their own life review. This is where they will be faced with the many things they have or have not done, or said, during the life they`ve just left behind.

This is believed to take up to forty hours when there has been a great deal of unfinished business in the life just exited.

For my own part, and whether or not my actions to do with his sister helped, I found that Peter, my husband, must have passed quickly through this life review as he was able to send through to me these miniature images of his etheric self, already healing, just six hours after his death.

Death is experienced as a bursting bubble of light energy, a sense of flow and freedom which lifts and releases the core etheric from the weight, restriction and boundaries of the physical shell. This little light burst ~ having hovered for a short while to reconnoitre with the effects taking place around the now lifeless physical body below ~ climbs and lifts through areas and channels of shaded to brighter light.

There is bound to be confusion and a sense of searching around to try to gain some kind of understanding, or control, over what has just happened. And yet one thing is certain, that all the physical pain has now gone for good, and the weight of the physical has now cleared ~ what a relief!

Sam: I must admit I like to hear that because my father had cancer and was in such pain so it must have felt wonderful to let all of that go.

Oh yes and a beautiful journey is waiting. The Inka believed they would immediately travel along the Milky Way to the stars, and the ancient Egyptians also felt that the celestial heavens would take them on a journey above the horizon.

Death is a lifting away to become one with all fields of energy where light is the sole survivor of any importance. Now we become our true twin selves as the physical body is transcended. Now there is an opening up into the other world of the etheric where levels of wisdom and knowledge appear.

The subtle light energy departs from the physical yet is still very much aware and has the ability to stay around, and in touch, with those left behind particularly if there is anything which needs to be communicated quickly.

Emmanuel Swedenborg came in touch with spirits who gave him some insight into the experience of death. He described this experience as::`still man does not die but is only separated from the corporeal part which was of use to him in the world.

Man, when he dies, only passes from one world into another.`

Ether body appearances

`After my husband, Stan, died he just came back one time and stood in front of me, watching me. I couldn`t speak, but he didn`t seem to want to talk. It was just as though he wanted me to know he was there, and okay, ` she says.

`He did this several times, just to make me aware of his presence. He looked younger than the age of sixty which was what he was when he died, but his clothes were familiar and he almost seemed to have substance as if he still existed in our world, somehow.

On one particular day he stood right beside a picture of my mother ~ who had been unwell for a while ~ and then he seemed to move to stand right by the phone. I suddenly felt this urge to ring Mum, it was as though he was telling me to do this.

I went to the phone and dialled her number and Stan immediately disappeared. But there was no reply to the phone and Mum always answered the phone, it was her life line ever since she was ill.

So I knew something was wrong, seriously wrong. I got in her car and took the fifteen minute drive to her house. It was a dull grey day and there were no lights showing at all from inside the house. Frantically, calling out, I unlocked the door with my own key and rushed through the hall, looking in the kitchen. `Mum, mum, where are you? Are you okay? Why don`t you answer the phone? `

And then I went into the sitting room and there she was, lying distraught and sobbing her heart out so she could hardly speak, she was on the floor with her leg all twisted up behind her.

Once I`d called in the ambulance and she was safely on her way to the hospital Mum managed to tell me: `I fell and couldn`t get to the phone, I couldn`t get help and I didn`t know what to do. `

`When did it happen, Mum? `

`Oh I don`t know but it can`t have been more than twenty minutes before you came though it felt like forever. I thought I was going to die there on the floor, and that nobody cared, nobody came. `

`Oh but I did come, Mum, and it was because somebody told me, in his own way, that I should come to help you. He must have told me at exactly the time it happened. `

Although, despite Mum`s curious look, I never did tell her just who had passed on the message in his own special way. `

Amber still reckons she can sense her grandmother`s presence sitting knitting up in her loft, just being around and present, in the ether, in her energy field, to see she`s okay, keep an eye on things as she did when she was alive.

Ellen found that after her father died she went on holiday to Ibiza and awoke just before dawn and was immediately aware of a glowing energy in the room which now contained both her parents ~ her mother had died a year before ~ standing with arms outstretched. She could feel a great sense of love coming from both of them although her father said she must not touch them as their energy was not stable.

John and Magggie set up a pact during life that they would prove if either of them died that they were still able to get in contact with the other. Each hid a specific object without telling the other one where it was and vowed to come back and tell the remaining partner after death. Maggie died first and did manage to tell John to go to the wardrobe and find in her coat pocket a photograph of him, and this was on the very day when, amidst much sadness, he had realised that he had to finally clear out all her clothes and this was just in time, before he had thrown her coat away.

He knew then, definitely, that she was still around.

Thirty year old Tania says: `My dad is definitely still with me in the house, even though he has died, because I keep hearing his footsteps going from one room to another, steadily, and then going up stairs.

And wherever I hear the footsteps the light switches on in that one particular room where the footsteps have stopped, temporarily, though he never switches the light off again afterwards. `

Maureen now lives in New Zealand but her mother, after she died, keeps coming back about every two months and switches on all the lights in the house. The first time it happened Colin, Maureen`s husband, said `I think that must be your mother` and Maureen agreed. `I think you`re right let`s see what happens` she said. `Mother is that you ~ are you proving you`re back here with us? ` At this point the lights flickered, buzzed, and then all went out throughout the whole house so that the two couldn`t help but know that it was definitely Mother just coming back to make sure they know she is still around in their house in New Zealand.

Two thirds of widows and widowers report seeing a close relative after death and eighty per cent gain some sense of their presence in the weeks and months following their loss.

Corah`s twenty six year old fiancee set off to Cumbria on a field trip without her. `He just said he needed some space, ` she reports, `although I knew the whole thing felt all wrong. I don`t know what I`d done or why he felt he had to get away and now I`ll never know because while he was walking in the mountains something did go wrong. I didn`t hear from him for a whole twenty four hours and I know the reception on the mobile might not have been very good up there but I was worried. I just knew something had happened to him.

In fact I knew more than that. I sensed he had fallen somehow in the mountains and that he had scratched his face on the way down, on some sharp bushes.

Of course I called out the rescue service and all I could tell them was that I knew he had these scratch marks just below his left eye, tearing right into his skin.

They said this was very helpful as it could assist them in narrowing down their search. They went to a particular area which was thick with prickly bushes

He was found later that day and there had been some thorny bushes at the place, on the mountain, from where he must have fallen. But even when they had told me the worst, that he was dead and I was making my way up to be with him, he managed to connect through to me, through all the layers of shock and grief. I had no idea I was psychic but he was able to tell me that the body is nothing and it doesn`t matter whether it is torn and broken or not because he didn`t need it any more.

He kept on telling me, over and over again, that he would always be with me from now on, and he would always love me and he was so sorry he had gone off like that. I never did find out why he did feel the need to disappear but at least I was able to give his rescuers an idea about the area where they would find him or they might never have found his body as he had gone away from the rest of the people on that field trip.

We had only been engaged for a year but I will never forget him, he is always here with me. `

Jenny was looking at the sky and thinking about her friend, Pat, who had died. She asked Pat to send a shooting star across the sky to prove they were still in contact. ` Pat did that for me, ` Jenny says, ` immediately a shooting star leapt across the sky.

Holograms exist throughout nature and for a hologram to appear there has to be an input of light. Every cell in the human body contains enough genetic information to create a clone, or a duplicate of the body, and it is known that this holographic effect happens because of the presence of a controlling electro magnetic field.

Chapter Nine

What happens to Jack when he DIES?

Sam: So can we ourselves have any influence at all about what happens around us as we die?

Jack will tell you. He was seventy nine years old and he also had cancer. They had done everything they could for him but now, after all the chemo and drugs, he had been told that he probably only had six months to live, at the most.

On January the fifth he was surprised to feel better, having been in pain for so long, and where he had not been very interested in eating or food, on this particular day he suddenly found he wanted to eat more.

In fact he felt better than he had for a long time, and he seemed to have more energy. Normally taking the dog for a walk was a chore but on this day he needed that walk.

And he couldn`t believe how good it felt, finding himself resolving to take a longer walk from now on despite some very unfriendly weather. It was very frosty and the temperatures had dropped dramatically ever since Christmas.

But he repeated the exercise on January the sixth. He was still eating more than he had been before and his energy was definitely better although the pains were growing more insistent again.

In the evening of this day he began to feel very light headed and, when his eyes were shut, and even when they were open, there were strange transparent shapes moving around behind his range of vision. Putting this down to his already failing eyesight he thought no more about it, and decided he had probably had too much exercise so would only go down to the pond on the next day.

January the seventh and Jack set off, well wrapped up, with

Bounder his beloved basset hound and they went as far as the pond. Jack`s energy was definitely lowering now and he was aware of all kinds of aches and pains he had never felt before, and he began to feel very weary. At just this minute Bounder saw another dog he liked and set off using the fastest route possible to reach his friend.

Unfortunately for Jack this route was right across the iced up pond although the temperature had been rising slightly, today, and the ice was beginning to crack. Suddenly, to Jack`s horror, he could see that Bounder was in difficulty having fallen through the ice and now he was howling and panicking, completely unable to get out.

The old man set off warily across the ice, there was no choice but to save his lifelong companion but he did feel so weak, and though he just managed to grasp the dog`s lead in a firm grip, hopefully to pull him out, he knew he didn`t really have the strength.

Suddenly the ice beneath his own feet cracked and fell apart and he fell through. He was very fragile and scarcely able to struggle though he kept hold determinedly on the dog`s long lead, not even noticing that by now Bounder had managed to free himself and climb back up to the safety of the ice from where he was now barking loudly, and people were running to try to help

Jack`s surrounding illuminated energy field now begins changing dramatically as he nears death. The water is too cold and he can`t hang on and, although he is no longer aware of the changes going on around and through him, the colours in his surrounding etheric outline change and lessen in intensity, gradually becoming paler, shrinking to a faint tinge.

As Jack`s brain begins closing down he just manages to feel this urgent need to ask God for forgiveness for all the times he neglected his wife, Mary, for his failure to be

understanding, and for the fallout with his brother which had left them not speaking for many years.

Jack is now feeling great discomfort at the strangeness of what is happening to him rather than any sense of his former pains. He feels disorientated, trying to regain control of some of his bodily functions, but they are all beyond him now and yet there is a great sense of love welling up inside him. Love for everything and everyone, perhaps even for himself?

Time, for him, feels as though it has stopped completely, he is right out beyond time and has no awareness of those who are already close to helping him, trying to save him.

He has no realisation but the echoing energy outline around him weakens to an etherial glow, already diluting to nothing. The spirit, which has been animating his body, is ready to depart from the physical shell and lift up through different etheric levels, choosing to exit from the crown of his head. Could anyone but see the subtle energy which has surrounded him as his twin body through life, this now begins to appear like a veil covering, filling with light as his soul lifts away.

Instead of being physically disorientated, as his spirit soul lifts into the Ether, Jack is aware of a vibrant burst of intense light immediately completely releasing him from his physical weight and boundaries. Like a brilliant shining star he is lifting up some twenty feet to hover above that now lifeless body lying down below, the cord of connection is broken and he can realise all that is going on so frantically as two men and a woman gradually lift his now lifeless physical shell out of the ice, but he is also very aware that he is still clutching hold of Bounder who is by now barking manically.

Jack needs to know that Bounder will be okay. He is aware that one of the men is already trying to untie the lifeless fingers still clutching on to that lead to take control of the dog, and he can hear the man shouting: `Get that barking

mongrel out of the way, I don`t care where it goes I don`t want it attacking me for trying to save its owner! `

Concentrating and leaning through his etheric energy field, Jack directs a strong intention straight towards the woman to seep and flow through the levels of her own surrounding etheric energy fields. His etheric energy reaches out to connect with her. She must make certain Bounder is safe.

`Look, I`ll take him, I`ll go to a dog`s home and make sure he will be looked after by somebody. He must be feeling a great sense of loss at this time, ` and there is so much understanding, love and conviction in her voice that Jack can send her through a welter of love before moving on to the next part of his journey.

He is moving further and further out into the cosmos, but as he does so he`s aware of a passageway or corridor which he gradually passes through, noticing to left and right varying degrees of shade and light. Now he begins his life review and all and every action he has ever taken in this recently released lifetime, and every word spoken together with each intention will be replayed and shown to him. Now he needs to learn where he has failed or when he used too much negative energy in his just passed life.

The experience of death is a gentle process which involves the simple act of passing through different levels and layers of our own and universal energy. This is an experience which takes the essence of the spirit beyond the physical pain and out into an etheric other world filled with overflowing light energy. Light is, ultimately, the true essence of all energy and death itself is nothing at all.

Having looked at Jack`s experience of death, it might be right to look at how other people experience the event when their loved one dies:

Sometimes we, too, experience what they are going through.

For instance Barnie, when his grandfather was dying, was sitting in the hospital with his mother and she reached out to hold her father`s hand to help ease his pain. Barnie says: `She told me later that while she was sitting there she could feel what he was feeling and that there was this kind of creeping pain building up and up, and she felt he was nearing death.

Then she stood up and said she had to go to the cloakroom and so I took over and held grandfather`s hand. I had no idea what my mother had experienced till later but, sure enough, at the time I could feel these same feelings as he must have been feeling. There was such tension running through him and I could feel that inner pressure building and then, suddenly, it all released and there was this feeling that passed through his hand, to mine, that was filled with a flowing calm.

I could hear him speaking to me and he was saying just the words: `loving calm,` but as I looked into his face I knew it was over and he had gone. And I think that message that came through to me happened as he was passing over. `

My mother came back and was distraught that she had missed his last moments, but I tried to convey to her that he had sent a message through to both of us in his words of `loving calm` and this did help her because they were not words I would ever have used myself.

Parcelsus, from the sixteenth century, found something similar and stated: `The vital force is not enclosed in man but radiates round him like a luminous sphere and it may be made to act at a distance`.

Experiences of the deceased affect energy of those left behind

I, personally, have had to undergo two or three occasions where I have had, after his death, to re-experience my husband`s pain and the explosion which was taking place inside his body leading up to the moment he died. The cause was an aortic aneurysm so that there would have been a massive build up of acid between his chest and stomach, and pain around the side of his chest or around his back, maybe also his flank..

On two occasions since my husband died I have suddenly found myself subject to completely unexpected and exploding pain and acid reflux feelings of turmoil, and twisting uncomfortable sensations around this same area between the abdomen and chest, and intense almost unbearable pain on the left hand side. I have had to undergo this pressure and pain for up to two hours wondering whether and how it would ever end.

On the first occasion I managed to help the pain and acute discomfort of the boiling bubbling sensation inside by the feeling that my husband was sending a beam or level of light into my energy to calm the whole feeling. On the second occasion I only managed to make it subside when he seemed to be telling me to feel a sense of forgiving love, both for myself and for him, and then the pain toppled over the crescendo and eased down and away.

This whole experience was like some kind of transformation which, it seemed, was very necessary for me to undergo.

With my own mother, I had no idea she was seriously ill whilst she was holidaying with her sister in Ibiza. My father phoned and said she was ill and would I fly over. We drove to Heathrow in half the time it usually took and every single traffic light was green. I had no ticket as it was being arranged by a friend, yet they held the plane from taking off just for me.

The moment the plane took off, as I was looking out of the window, and having no idea that she had died, I found myself going back with my mother, through the events and happenings in **her** life, and I now know this must have been her life review.

When the plane landed my father said she had died and I told him I knew, not only that she had died, but exactly the moment it happened because I was right there with her.

Ether Communication

Anita was flying with her husband, Edward, and their seven year old son Thomas who was so excited to be taking a short flight in a cessna, during their holiday in South America.

`But, ` she tells me, ` the flight was to end in tragedy and was forced to come down in a wasted area. It was terrifying, and both Edward and I were seriously injured but we managed to scramble around frantically to find Thomas.

When we found him, under some plane debris, he was obviously dead and I was screaming and screaming, I couldn`t believe this happened from a simple trip on a family holiday. The pilot was dead, too, but when the rescuers came and found us, they quickly hurried Thomas`s body away to a nearby hospital, and took us separately to the same hospital.

We kept asking them how he had died? They told us it was because of the injuries he had received to his abdomen when he had impacted, during the crash, with the seat in front, and this caused a gaping wound from which he had lost a lot of blood.

When we had recovered a little Edward and I went back to the crash site just before the investigation into the cause of the crash and the final cause of Thomas`s death was established. We somehow felt we would be nearer to him there than in the hospital where his body was.

And as soon as I approached the remains of that plane and went around to the side where Thomas had been lying, I was suddenly screaming from a sharp pain in my neck. I was crying out with this intense pain, put my hand to the back of my neck and then felt pain right through me, all the way down my spine and through my limbs.

Then I felt myself unable to scream or cry out any more and I fell down on the ground and couldn`t move. `Anita what`s happening? What is it, please, please, are you okay?` I gradually became aware of Edward trying to speak to me, needing me to respond but I couldn`t, it took a long while for me to come back up from what felt like the bottom of a pit where I couldn`t move.

Yet there was something of inestimable value in that journey back upwards for me.

Thomas`s voice, his laughing joyful voice, filled with energy, more even than he had ever had in life. I could hear his voice but I could only see him as a point of light though he was right there with me and he was telling me: `My neck! The impact broke my neck and severed all the nerves to my limbs and brain ~ that`s what killed me, mama, but I`m free, I`m so light and free and I`m so glad you took me on that journey. `

That light was so bright and shining, Thomas had always loved everything that had light in it and sparkled for him.

Gradually I was able to tell Edward the story, and there was a change in the whole way I felt about myself. All the pain from my neck, spine and limbs had gone and where, before, I had been regretting and berating myself so much for ever having suggested the short flight, suddenly I felt it was meant to be and was something that was going to happen. Thomas was telling me that he was going to die on that day whatever we had done differently.

And when we got back to the hospital the results from the post mortem were available, telling us he died, not from the wound to his stomach, but from a broken neck which had severed all the nerves in his spinal cord. `

Chapter Ten

What makes a PSYCHIC psychic?

Sam: Some people are psychic and know what`s coming. So with this twinself energy thing going on can we all be psychic?

You`re right, Sam, our ether twinlightself gives us access to another level of energy entirely. Our extra ether fields make every level and dimension of energy accessible to every one of us, and it is from the etheric level that all kinds of psychic or inexplicable happenings occur.

We could all tap into our gifts of intuition, clairvoyance, psychic vision or having a remote effect on the energy of others

To be psychic you just have to tune in to your extra wave length of fast vibrating energy, like tuning in to a radio.

The same holds true for all mediums, tarot card readers, or anyone with psychokinetic or telepathic abilities to know what someone else is thinking. People like Derren Brown and Uri Geller use their extra power level to connect with messages flying around in the Ether, normally beyond conscious thinking

Sam: I`ve read that when someone performs psychic surgery they don`t touch the person but work just outside the body on the problem areas, so how does that work?

Psychic surgeons draw out negative blockages from our energetic body which could cause the complaint or disease. This could be a better way of healing than using drugs.

There are well known psychic surgeons in this country such as Stephen Turoff ~ who works from Chelmsford ~ and he seems to enter the body to remove different formations like tumours or blood clots. He is described as working through different dimensions. After the proceedure, a red mark is left on the skin, like a scar, which disappears after a few days.

What these surgeons are doing is making surgical changes in and through the energetic double body to reflect in the physical

In Stephen Turoff`s case a certain Dr Kahn is said to take control of his arms and hands during the five minute operation. He works through non material fields, pastel lights are seen to descend into patients` bodies. Sacred ash forms on objects or people in the surgery, towels and sheets can turn pink.

This man, known as a gentle giant, describes himself as an instrument through whom others can work. For them the physical body represents vibrations of subatomic particles rather than any kind of physical barrier.

There are many psychic surgeons in places like the Phillippines and Brazil who perform operations with their bare hands over the body and with no implements to help them make cuts or incisions. They remove the pathological matter and seal up the skin again to leave no trace of a scar.

When these psychic surgeons are working the skin softens to become more fluid so that etheric energy can flow through.

Sam: But how do they do this and make the connection?

What they`re actually doing is using the frontal lobes of their own brains and working through the etheric level of energy, guided by the wisdom of those in the etheric world. They are, in fact, particularly using the right temporal lobe.

There`s a magic world in there, in this lobe of the brain, to immediately give us access to timeless spaceless reality of the invisible parallel world. This lobe has its own consciousness and communicates through pictures and holographic images.

What they do is use their third eye window, behind the forehead to make their own connection to this other dimension.

This right temporal lobe is also used by mediums to tap straight in to the Ether World. Now spirits beyond our world connect through them to share vital messages with us here.

Sam: Can anyone use their right temporal lobe like this?

It does take practice. Some people are blessed with an extra level of spiritual sight ~ by connecting through pineal and pituitary glands ~ but there are exercises which can help all of us to strengthen our inner `seeing` ability, meditation, for a start, to clear the inner chattering of the conscious mind.

Or there are more complicated things called brainwave stimulators which can be used. Otherwise you could use incense or try increasing your own memory retaining abilities and powers of intuition to exercise the right temporal lobe.

Sam: My memory is not very good so how do I do this?

By trying something as simple as guessing which card will come up when you have previously turned over a whole pack of cards to lie face down on a table.

Or you could ask someone to draw a picture without your seeing what it is, and then try to guess what they`ve drawn. Anything which calms and quietens that overactive conscious part of your mind that is normally so involved in the demands of daily living. It is always your conscious mind which stops you from realising your inner hidden powers.

This right temporal lobe of the brain is very powerful in other ways such as producing near death experiences. This increases the inner response to electromagnetic energy and people have more psychic experiences after an NDE.

Sam: I`d rather try something simpler.

As you exercise the frontal lobes of the brain, neural receptors ~ which help you analyse any energy messages you receive like your father connecting to your energy fields ~ stimulate.

Through the unseen parallel world everything and anything is always possible. ETHER ENERGY EXISTS EVERYWHERE AND IS THE KEY TO EVERY PARANORMAL EVENT

Sam: Do we have extra stores of ether in the body?

The liver, spleen and pancreas receive most of the etheric energy in our bodies. This flow connects from the base of the skull straight up and out to other dimensions. Of course this is the way we leave when we die to become wholly our ether twin

We spend so much time running away from our inherently magical energetic abilities but these could help our struggle through life, as we force ourselves to learn by mistakes.

We need to remember our outer extra energy body which protects our energy and charges up our life force. When we become negatively emotional, our shining outline diminishes shrinks and blocks up instead of expanding outwards..

We dull and dim our light input which affects the light reaching our cells. This is liable to bring in illness and disease.

One way for anyone with psychic tendencies to learn to expand their gift is by practice and working to further this ability by attending workshops which concentrate on exercising the right temporal lobe of the brain.

I attended one of these workshops, run by Debbie, who says we all have this gift but we can either use it or lose it. Various exercises are undertaken to push and promote our psychic abilities. At one point Debbie suggested each person try to sense or feel a presence of spirit energy standing behind them. ***This is definitely a great way to start on the path of trying to sense the energy of a close loved one who is now wholly in spirit or their etheric body.***

After this exercise ~ where I found myself in contact with a curly headed cousin, who had died at a young age, and seemed to have a message about the allergies and health in my family ~ Debbie asked us all to discuss what had happened to us, individually. She then told me that she, herself, could sense an energy, in spirit, close to me.

She felt this was my husband in early years, possibly around the nineteen seventies because of the way he was dressed. She said he had lots of dark curly hair and that he was lifting his hair up to show his sideburns.

Yes I could remember that he did have long and heavy sideburns and dark curly hair so I was with her so far, but then she said that he was wearing these big goggle type black glasses with a gold rim right around them. And I could not, for the life of me, remember any such glasses or envisage Peter as having worn them.

She went on to describe his hairstyle as being `punk` and that he was wearing something in dusky pink ~ again not like him ~ and that he was wearing a short sleeved shirt ~ something he seldom wore. Though she couldn`t see his eyes it was those dark glasses she noticed as he kept coming up and peering at her through them.

I went home that night not sure what was happening here but something pulled me towards our vast collection of photographs. However, I had little hope of finding Peter wearing these strange and, for him, unusual things.

Before long I found THE picture! In the nineteen eighties we had been at a themed party where we had to be dressed as punks or rockers. There he is wearing a black punk wig ~ clearly showing sideburns beneath ~ and he has a pink scarf round his neck, he is also wearing a short sleeve shirt.

The most important item, though, must be those giant goggle like glasses he wears, with their gold outer rim!

On telling Debbie later about this photo she found it very funny and said: `Ha, ha, he certainly makes us work to get our proof that he is still around. `

This is so true but so much more rewarding when the truth and evidence does come through. Given the very deep nature of this man he would never have set out to make anything too

easy. In life he had trouble reaching down to gain his inner knowledge so, after death, he would prefer not to give away his secrets too easily.

Peter appears for me, through Debbie, three times in all and each time he appears at an entirely different age, and time, in his just passed life. Yet again this gives further proof that no medium comes by their information too easily.

Sam: Yes you would have thought she would just see him later on, closer to his death.

Well as you will see that did happen and, at the end of the book he will appear as he was over forty years ago, on the night we first met. HE HAS TO BE GIVING THIS INFORMATION THROUGH DEBBIE, TO ME, OR ELSE WHERE DOES IT COME FROM?

Sam: I gather his health broke down at the end from a steady build up. Is there any was to release our negative energy to stop this from happening?

Yes, definitely, in various ways Sam. Firstly if we continually wrap ourselves and concentrate all our energy through negative feelings and thoughts, anger, hatred, guilt or fear, these feelings expand out through our personal light energy field, out to the world, and bring back more of the same.

Strangely, things like colds and catarrh can help this clear.

Sam: Colds? That doesn`t make sense, how can that happen?

Colds nudge our inner supplies of ether energy ~ as a fluid in our body ~ into becoming more substantial by producing heavier mucous. This is a great way for our body to release our emotional negativity. Think of an overflow pipe trying to release too much tension.

By having a cold we are cleansing ourselves from our inner negative build up in a tangible way. Gradually, this begins to clear any blocks we`ve placed on our inner ether energy. Ether turns from a fluid into a substance and can be released by coughing or blowing the nose.

Sam: So taking all those pills and potions to try to stop the symptoms is not helping?

No, we`re just blocking ourselves up again. Having a temperature produces the same effect in that we reach for the paracetamol ~ our energy becomes more opaque ~ reduce the temperature and halt our body`s natural way of healing. T**his is not what the body wants.**

When we do have flu, viruses, colds or catarrh we could be clearing our negativity.

Where people become depressed after flu this is because they have stoppered up the natural release of the inner ether fluid.

Sam: Our ether body could be inner and outer nurse or healer?

Yes, that`s it, we have a surrounding level or an energetic vibe which only wants to help us. This is part of a whole universal flow of lighter, brighter energy and we could be tapping in to this resource at any time, but we`ll look more into healing later.

Sam: *Hey, so that`s what they mean when they talk about something lifting your spirits?*

Oh, yes, in fact those who look at life with a positive smile on their face or an upbeat attitude to life suffer far fewer colds because they don`t have to keep releasing negativity. If they do come down with a cold they`ll get over it far more quickly because they`ve found this knack of keeping their inner etheric flowing and glowing.

We need to live life not just ethically but etherically through our outer twin body.

My husband died from an aortic aneurysm resulting from having athersclerosis or narrowing of the arteries. One particular cause for this was said to be: `having a difficulty with handling anger`. And this is true, he carried an inner sense of anger and injustice across the last seventeen years of his life, and he had pushed anger down into his arteries to form a block to the free flow of his life force energy.

Sam: I can see how this affects all kinds of illnesses but if we have a virus ~ not just a cold where the mucous is obvious ~ how, then, do we turn that fluid back into a state of flowing etheric energy? What could your husband have done?

Okay so we are physical beings, living in physical bodies, surrounded by our own light energy field. If we just begin projecting light bright positive thoughts and feelings out through this field, the field expands to uplift our inner and outer ether vitality.

The greater the charge of vital force within and around our physical body, the faster the vibrations of our energy and the less need we have for slow vibrational illness or disease.

Increase the love in the heart and out through your own light energy field. In fact there is increased electro magnetic radiation around the heart. Our hearts are a great power source to lift our lives to a higher faster vibrational frequency, and love travels on a faster vibration than other emotion can do.

Sam: Can we be either a high or low frequency person?

Yes because how we feel is how we vibrate. This is the life vibe we`re on. The more of this high fast light energy we feed through from our outer twinself, the faster our vibration will be. Currently we mostly live life on a low frequency vibration.

The cells organs and organisms inside us resonate to different etheric frequencies as energy transmits through the different levels in our bodies, and the echo always generates out from us.

All kinds of outside influences resonate to different frequencies, through the Ether. Some of these will be disharmonious to our own energy field. In various ways they could cause us to harm or gradually destroy ourselves. They drag us down to low frequencies whether it is our fault or someone else`s doesn`t matter in the end.

But we always have this outer twinlight self working for us as our transparent source of energy.

Sam: So to `step out of yourself` means into your twin?

Yes and if we could see ourselves in a transparent plastic raincoat as an image of this twin then the rain wouldn`t get in.

Sam: Okay so we need to keep our light outline sunny?

Definitely! This is what anyone who dies from our lives keeps trying to tell us. THE GREAT SECRET THEY WANT US TO SHARE LIES IN OUR OUTER ENERGY.

But when a loved one dies and we drown in layers of grief they can no longer contact us through low energy vibrations. They currently exist in such high energy frequencies there is no way through when we are swamped by negativity.

Healing tip: massage your etheric outline just beyond your skin

Sam: Okay I`m beginning to see how Dad is contacting me but I could now do with more evidence from other people.

Right then this is the time to learn more about Debbie and how she connects with other world energies.

Chapter Eleven

Interview with DEBBIE the medium

It is really interesting to meet the bubbly blonde Debbie Dean as an intriguing, comforting and genuinely caring person who uses her psychic and intuitive gifts, as a medium, to reassure countless numbers of people that their deceased loved ones are still `alive`.......... through another world of energy.

As well as undertaking her meaningful, individual sittings, Debbie also recreates astonishing likenesses through her spiritual portraits. These are images, channelled through to her, of the person who has died.

She may say she lacks artistic ability but these portraits are incredible and created very rapidly by her own hand ~ in as little as nine seconds. When she shows me some of the images she achieves, beside original photographs, the likeness is undeniable.

Debbie`s whole mission in life is to bring comfort to so many people as she passes on messages, images, feelings and words from those now existing in the spirit world. Over and again she brings evidence that the deceased loved one is still very much around in our energy as she tells how **`death is a process which merely takes the physical body.`**

Debbie describes how there is no such thing as fabric in the spirit world so that when spirits don specific clothing, or assume a particular appearance, this is merely for those left behind so that they can recognise their loved one who has, by now, assumed a spiritual energy shape This even applies with such recognisable items as glasses which spirit can wear to appear to her ~ in turn to be recognisable to their family ~ but only for this reason as they no longer need glasses to see!

She is also able to undertake all kinds of paranormal investigations to rid people of any unwanted energies in their homes.`But only when everything else fails, and when it is time to accept that this is a paranormal happening` she explains.

If you look on her website you can see a photo, taken at a graveside, which shows a face and also a kneeling figure which is similar to what Debbie can see, most of the time. She is constantly aware of spirit `presences` which exist alongside the physical presence of people.

`This comes as a natural gift to me and, even from the age of four years old, I could see and sense having these other people around, moving across and through my life. These were people in `spirit` who were not visible in the material world.

And I always thought that everyone else could see them too but, as a teenager, I found I had to become a bit more reserved about it all, and keep it to myself since others didn`t understand what I was saying or seeing.

But this ability to see a `hidden world` didn`t go away and it was only as the years passed that I began to realise how I could help people who were desperately seeking some kind of supporting comfort, when they`d lost someone they loved. `

And what comfort she gives! There are so many messages that she can pass on during individual sittings or public demonstrations, and sometimes in ordinary everyday circumstances ~ as we will see ~ for this is a sitter who practices from an honest point of view, in a bid to help people. She wants them to be able to relate to what she can see as their loved ones connect with her from the other world.

There is no sense of urgency but those who exist in the spirit world want to share their experience of their continuing existence with those they have left behind. And this they are able to do, thanks to Debbie, to give a new sense of hope to those who thought they would never get their lives back on track. She gives information only the deceased could have known.

But this medium does give out warnings because there are those who are not so meticulous in their mediumship practices. There are some who pass on messages which can disturb or bring fear to people and this deeply concerns her.

She begs people to be careful of the few dodgy mediums around and suggests people always only visit a medium specifically recommended to them by friends or local Spiritualist church.

`One woman came to see me when she was in a right old state, Debbie says, `because 22 years before she had been to see a less than authentic medium who told her she would have a child, over the next few months, but that he wouldn`t live for very long.

So this poor woman was in torment for, despite her son having now reached 22, she couldn`t rest as she was expecting to lose him at any moment.

What I did was to bring forward a relation, in spirit, whom the woman trusted to bring messages to show that the son`s life would continue on well past 22, and that he would be okay.

I myself had an out of body experience in the early days, just when my son was born, and my heart stopped beating. Suddenly I found myself in another level of energy that I don`t have the words to describe, but I was well aware of what was going on with my physical body, as well as in the next room where they were concentrating on my son.

From whatever level of energy I found myself ~ by being out of my body ~ I could still read the name badges of those who were with my son. When the overwhelming need to be with him pulled me back into my body, and into life again, I could give the names of the people who had been working on him, even though they were in a different room to me.

I used to be a midwife and I delivered many babies, and I could always see this beautiful aura which would come through first before the baby was born.

Where the aura of an adult is an oval shape with a slight point at the top, in babies I could still see the aura with a trail leading off into the spirit world which they had just left. For me this proves a close connection between spirit world and our own.

Sometimes it is a bit exhausting to be a medium, ` she tells me, ` with so many people continually wanting messages and signs from you. This can be especially tiring when people demand specific people to come through, for them, or when they expect answers to definite questions. I have to tell them I have no control over what is happening in the spirit world.

The spirits choose to come through to make contact with their loved ones, and THEY choose what they will say or show as evidence of who they are. Any medium is just the one in the middle and its not up to them to decide, but for the spirits themselves to make things happen. Life will always be unexpected for anyone with mediumistic abilities. `

Debbie also confirms that for those who are married to mediums life is not always going to be easy, especially in her case where she often sees people around in spirit energy. `This does make it difficult for my husband when we are out and he wants to hold my full attention, ` she confirms.

`One time, ` she says, `I went out for a meal in Brighton, with my husband, in an area near the Kings Head pub, in the Brighton Lanes and I became aware of a woman at another table whose father, as spirit, was standing right next to her, trying to communicate his presence.

My husband told me not to interrupt or become involved. But after our meal we went to several places around Brighton and every time, wherever we went, there she was again, this woman with father alongside, urging her to be aware of his presence. I so much wanted to tell her what was happening.

But I managed to resist, every time, until the last time when we ended up on the beach and there she was, plus father, again.

This was too much and I just had to go over to the woman and say: `Excuse me, I`m sure you`ll think I`m crazy but I have to tell you that I`m a medium.` `Oh I see,` said the woman, stepping back slightly.

But whilst sensing this resistence, I felt I had to continue: `And I have something urgent to tell you because I saw you, in the restaurant, and I could see your father standing beside you, leaning over towards you wanting you to know he was there.`

Now the woman was overwhelmed with gratitude. ` Thank you so much, ` she said, `my father died a year ago and these were exactly the places I used to come to with him. It is so good to know he`s okay, and that he`s still around me. Can I pay you for your trouble? `

`No I don`t want anything, I just want you to know that your father is here with you. `

Mentally, without saying so, I now urged the woman to take her father with her and go. During the rest of the afternoon in Brighton we neither saw the woman or her father again. This made me realise that my mission in this instance was fulfilled. `

With her gifts as a spiritual portrait artist, some of her experiences bring out totally unexpected reactions from people. Whilst discussing, with her, the fact that some who move into the spirit world seem to undergo their healing very quickly, where others can take years for their healing to be completed, Debbie tells me about one time when she was working with another medium on stage.

`Whilst the other medium was connecting with and relaying facts about what spirit was telling her, without knowing who the message was for I was drawing the portrait. A woman came up and said: `That`s my husband, he has just died and tomorrow is his funeral.` The woman went off happily with the portrait, and both myself and the other medium realised that he must have undertaken his healing process quickly to be able to come through so soon. The next day, at the funeral, the woman put the portrait on an easel for everyone to see.

`Oh that`s a good likeness of my brother, ` her brother in law came up to tell her, `when did he have that done? `

`Yesterday, ` the woman told him, the light of amusement playing behind her eyes.

`But he died a week ago, ` the brother in law said in confusion to which she simply answered: `Exactly.`

Debbie describes herself as clairsentient, as she believes most mediums are, and she works with her feelings as well as her inner vision. She explains that some mediums don`t see anything at all but rather that they are clairaudient and merely work with what they hear. She has always been described by her family as like a little butterfly who floats off somewhere.

When I ask her how she sees spirit she tells me that: ` I see spirit as I see you, and I let them guide me. Sometimes I work solely on what I feel and can feel spirit working with the energy of and through my solar plexus.

Sometimes I receive fragmented messages with dates, names or a set of numbers which will connect somehow for the person experiencing the sitting. Or there might be key words where spirit communicates by working from their memory of when they were a physical being.

Spirit always contacts me. `I can`t dial them up, but I do believe that everybody is born with the gift of mediumship although it is up to us whether we use it or lose it. There are people who say they see nothing, or they don`t connect, so then I ask them: `Do you see your loved one in dreams? `

When they agree that they do I can explain to them: ` That is the way they choose to appear to you as you find it difficult to sense them on normal levels, so they have to approach you through your subconscious mind. They appear through your dreams as your own personal route of contact, or, otherwise through mediums who are just that, in the middle.

I don`t believe in coincidence, especially in connection with the spirit world where everything is happening specifically, to bring messages to us in our physical world.

We all have this physical overcoat ~ as our body ~ here in life and we leave this behind when we die. We come from source and it is to source that we return. `

When people ask her for her description of heaven and hell she tells them: `I believe that heaven is the spirit world to which we go when we die, and that hell is here in physical life where we are having to experience everything. Of course life can be beautiful but it can also be extremely testing. `

I need her take on the spirit world and carefully do not mention any of my own findings in my investigation into the world of ether energy.

`Where do you think the spirit world is? ` I ask her

`Oh I feel it runs parallel with us, here, for when we`ve finished with the overcoat of our physical body, and feel we can be free of the heaviness of it all, when we are ready to go back to source instead of being here, making the best of it. `

`How do you experience paranormal events? ` I question.

`Oh sometimes you can`t avoid or ignore them. There was a house, in Tilgate, where the mirror leapt off the wall and came straight towards me. This was a heavy mirror which should, logically, have fallen straight downwards but this one was definitely intended for me though fortunately it missed me.

Then there was the place where the door knob turned round right in front of me, and three other people, but nobody was around or touching the door. We all saw it but by the time one of us had reached down for his camera of course it stopped.

But there was nobody there at all, on either side of the door.

`So how do you deal with energies when they are not

welcome or wanted? ` I want to know.

`Oh you ask them to move on and they do. Sometimes I get this paranormal feeling in my solar plexus and I know the energy around has altered. Also spirits can pull on your clothing to make you notice them, though this happens more in sittings.Ghosts can`t make contact but spirits can and do. `

And this is the point where she suddenly starts asking me questions about my own husband. I never expected any contact to be made between Peter and Debbie so was quite surprised.

And I can hardly ignore what she is saying: `Was your husband losing his hair towards the end? ` She asks, and I admit that yes, to his eternal regret, he had lost a lot of hair.

And then she says: `And did he smoke? ` Well he certainly did, he smoked cigars which didn`t help his physical health at all, but he was defiant all the way through and wouldn`t give up so that they became like his signature.

Then she tells me: `Well he`s sitting over there in the corner, looking very happy with himself, and he has one knee crossed over the other and one hand on his hip. In the other hand is his cigar and he`s blowing smoke out from the corner of his mouth, like this, ` **and in that instant she manages to demonstrate his mannerisms exactly.**

We`re sitting in the outside area of the tea rooms, and she indicates a corner of rocks and stones where he could easily be sitting, though I can`t actually see him here with us.

At the beginning of our meeting I had answered a phone call from my daughter having suggested she might want to join us as we were near to where she worked. She is calling back to say she knows I was nervous about this meeting and is it because I had often been to the same tea rooms with her father? Also to say she can`t make it.

But far from being nervous, I now find myself filled with excitement, as must happen for so many people when they consult such an inspirational medium as Debbie. Peter obviously likes her too, and has no intention of my meeting her without his being present.

`He`s saying he would like to join us in a cup of tea though, for him, the spoon would stand up in it since he takes so much sugar, ` Debbie tells me and she is so right, **he would always have at least three spoons of sugar with his te**a.

`And he wants to be here with us and is so much enjoying our conversation, and now I can hear a pipe being tapped out and emptied on the table with this rapping sound, ` she demonstrates on the table. `Did he smoke a pipe? `

`No,` I can answer, `but his father did and was always rapping on the table with his pipe so he is around too? `

She confirms this and then goes on to tell me: `And Peter is showing me a jacket in a sort of fawn or beige colour, and this is important to him, as is the number 72, was he 72 ?

`No he wasn`t, ` I tell her since he was three years short of that age, but on thinking around this number for a short while I suddenly realise that it must have been about 1972 when Peter finished the house he laboriously built for us, up in Essex, and of which he was so proud. It could be that he had been wearing that jacket around that time, I`ll check later.

I had been more used to seeing him dressed in black in recent years. `He had a very dry sense of humour, liking things like Monty Python, ` Debbie continues.

`Or Blackadder, ` I agree because this man was known for his dry sense of humour.

**`And people didn`t quite `get` him, couldn`t fathom him or understand him,** ` she tells me. THIS IS SO TRUE OF THIS MAN, NOBODY EVER UNDERSTOOD HIM AND THIS SUMS HIM UP COMPLETELY. Even my mother had said she couldn`t make him out at all.

Debbie is so on the button with all of this which slightly

unnerves me as I had thought it was just me who was in touch with him, though our daughter is sometimes, too.

Debbie goes on to tell me that one of her sons, when aged around two years, kept complaining that angel was around in his bedroom, an angel with a bald head.

Debbie didn`t understand this and asked him over again because somehow she had never visualised angels as having anything other than flowing hair.

But it was later on, when she was investigating with neighbours about who had lived in the house before, she learned there had been a young girl who had cancer, and was undergoing chemotherapy. And this made her lose her hair!

I ask again for more of a description as to how she sees people and she tells me: `It is more out of my peripheral vision which happens sometimes, and this is like when people are watching tv and they see something out of the corner of their eyes, as though someone is passing by, or lights are flashing by. This is a subconscious prompting.`

We go on to discuss about whether she feels that when our time comes to die there is no arguing with it. In fact she describes this as being: `All in our blueprint before we come in.

In fact some people, in spirit, tell me they want to thank their relatives for giving permission for them to leave because there are instances where people have to die on their own, or the pull from the relations sitting with them is too strong and this makes it more difficult to go.

I had one woman in a sitting who said she sat near her father`s bed, towards the end, for three full days and it was only when she left the room for a minute, just to get a drink, that he died and she couldn`t understand why. This could be one of those instances where the pull to hold on was too strong

And Debbie goes on to say that: `Science can try to deny all of these paranormal happenings and the very truth of how life goes on after we die physically, but they cannot deny that energy can never stop and has to go on, continuously, although it just changes its form. It is just like putting water in a kettle and then you have steam which dissolves in the air. This is just a change from one form to another. `

We discuss how so many people who profess not to believe yet find themselves describing certain children as `an old soul` or as `someone who has been here before`.

Debbie stresses how all the information she has been given comes to her from those who choose to appear in connection with one or other person. That she is not controlling this situation at all, it is up to spirit world, they bring her the truth.

`And this is the vitally important thing that all this information is authentic and able to help people. I, myself, did once try going to a supposed clairvoyant, and there were no rings on my fingers, and this woman kept looking at my hands and then described how sad it was that I had never met `the` man in my life`. And that I was obviously desperate for children but had never been able to have them.

So in the end I had to tell this woman that not only was I a mother of four, living with my husband who was `the` man of my life, but I was also a grandmother of two. But this makes me so sad that there are people giving out false information which is not necessary when there are such valid and true mediums who can really help, comfort and console people. We can bring the knowledge that the loved ones are still right here with us in spirit`.

Any nerves I might have had about this meeting have turned to excitement with all Debbie has been able to describe to me and the way Peter has chosen to join in our discussion.

I spend the evening searching for a photo of Peter wearing that fawn/beige jacket, in corduroy, that he was so adamantly showing to Debbie to relay to me. After much searching I find not one, but two, photos of him in that very jacket. One of the photos would have been in 1971, and the other one in 1975.

Then I search in his autobiography ~ yes despite only being 69 when he died, my husband had very helpfully written his own autobiography ~ to find out what was happening to him in 1972, something obviously so vital to act as a clue to be given to me by Debbie, to prove he was with us at tea.

And there it is! Written in hard copy Peter describes how it was, in 1972, that he and I moved in to his beloved house, the one which he himself had built and of which he was so proud.

I know that in latter years he always regretted not being able to build another house for me, and so this was the greatest message, and key, for him to pass on through Debbie to me.

It is just so fascinating to discover how Debbie has confirmed so much of what I have uncovered during my own investigations ~ with Sam`s help ~ into the unseen world of the etheric. This is especially so when she describes the place where the spirits go .... **a parallel world to our own from which they can reach out and be with us in our world.**

This is verification indeed. She sees the process of death as returning to our true spirit home, and spirit selves, having thrown off the overcoat we have worn during our physical lives, so that we may travel into this comforting other parallel world of continuous energy.

Debbie Dean is a certified medium and tutor belonging to the governing body of the United Spiritualists. She undertakes private sittings and public demonstrations. She believes we are all connected by unconditional love to those in the spirit realm. She is also a founder of the CPI, Crawley Paranormal Investigators and her website is: www.debbiedean.org.uk

Pamela`s strange experiences of the afterlife world

Pamela suffered through an inexplicable period of sadness and feelings of deep depression for no apparent reason at all. The feelings just hit her, suddenly, and she couldn`t get to grips with herself, or her life. There were feelings of sadness as though someone was trying to connect with her although she had no idea who it might be.

A friend, at her yoga class, suggested she should visit a certain Dr. McAll who was an unusual combination of being a member of the clergy, at the same time as being a therapist, and he asked her a very strange question: He asked: `Did your mother ever have any miscarriages? ` She couldn`t understand this one but confirmed that yes, her mother did have a miscarriage. He then went on to explain that her intense feelings of sadness could be coming from some member of her family who had died, but was not being acknowledged, and explained that it could be this child denied to her mother through the miscarriage.

The next step for them was to acknowledge this lost child, and clear the sense of distress that was still coming through to Pam from the energy of the one who would have been her brother or sister.

For a while Pam was fine, but then it happened again and she found herself trapped in exactly the same feelings, for no apparent reason. She was talking to her sister about this, their mother having died a while before, and Barbara said: `Oh, no, didn`t you know, she had two miscarriages not one. ` So that now Pam could, once again, acknowledge another of her would-be brothers or sisters, and she found immense relief in her feelings after this and she managed to release the pain from her mother too.

About this time she heard a story about a vicar and his wife, and how they had a child who had autism so that his

behaviour was unpredictable. However, his mother became pregnant and then, to her great consternation, she miscarried of a boy child. After this happened her son William`s behaviour reached extreme levels so that she could not take him out anywhere. All of which just made her own suffering even worse.

However, a day came when this woman and her husband went to visit their Bishop, in great distress because they could not get over their feelings of loss. And the Bishop explained that they needed to acknowledge the child she had miscarried, to give him a name and release him into the light energy of Jesus. Once having done this, they returned home where their unruly and out of control son, William, came up to them immediately and said he felt happy, had lots of good energy, now, and would not cause them any more problems.

He said he knew he had been difficult, recently, and it was all because of `the baby` who would have been his brother, but that the `baby` was happy now.

Pam obviously has certain psychic or mediumistic powers and at another time she found herself connecting with her cousin ~ who had been eighteen years old when he was killed in the war ~ feeling as though he was communicating with her from behind a glass screen. `In this way I felt I could empathise with his feelings but not actually feel them in myself, ` she says. `He was coming through as being very angry, asking for my help to gain peace and release.

He kept on repeating this and was complaining about how he felt he had been treated so badly, that he still couldn`t approve of wars or any need for the mass killings involved.

He was angry at the way he had to die, so suddenly, but he kept on appearing to me as a kind of energy echo, or a voice that almost appeared like a ghostly presence. But I

definitely recognised him and knew he was my cousin.

Gradually, I managed to calm him in all these repeated appearances because it was all getting too much for me to cope with. I found I could help him to move from the anger to a calmer more peaceful level. From here he could seek help to move on from the place where he seemed to be trapped between the worlds.

Very curiously, I had the chance to be regressed some time later and I really wanted to know why it was often men from the war zones who communicated with me. So that it wasn`t a great surprise to learn that, in a previous life in the First World War, I was a conscientious objector.

My grandmother committed suicide by putting her head in a gas oven and I also felt as though I went through the same experience with her. Afterwards my Gran got in touch to tell me why she had done it. She said she couldn`t cope and everyone had taken her so much for granted that she no longer felt she was an individual person. But she did tell me that she still felt so guilty, from where she was in the afterlife, that she needed someone, ie me, to know the reason for her having done this to herself. `

There were also a couple of Pam`s friends where the man died suddenly when playing tennis. `From the level of energy where he existed after death he knew that my energy was open and able to receive the one message which he desperately needed to share.

He wanted to connect with his wife, Sylvie, and tell her he was all right. He had deep regrets about not ever having had the chance to say goodbye to her. He kept urging me to write to Sylvie and tell her because he told me his wife was just not able or open enough to receive any kind of communication from him.

But he kept on getting in touch with me, and frankly it

was all becoming too much, and I was getting annoyed with all these appeals for help. I didn`t really want to mention anything to my friend, his wife, since I felt it would upset her over again, and so I kept quiet. And yet the husband insisted on tapping on my shoulder and kept on interrupting me, asking for me to contact Sylvie.

Finally I relented and wrote to Sylvie to explain that her husband was still feeling the guilt of never having said goodbye. In fact Sylvie was pleased to receive the message, it relieved her mind and then, at last, her husband felt free to move on, and he never did feel the need to contact me again.`

Chapter Twelve

A charge of ELECTRICITY

Sam: Is electricity involved when ether appearances happen?

In this universe, Sam, fields of energy vibrate in colour frequencies through sound and **light**, magnetic fields rotate, roll and react spontaneously with each other.

Now magentic fields cause energy eruptions in our world. Massive, multiple solar flares sweep the sun`s surface.
Radiant light power bursts through solar winds and charges of highly magnetic energy create across the air, and electro magnetic particles release to spin throughout the ether levels.

Sam: Can we feel this happening?

Since every particle is charged with force fields of electro magnetic energy this nourishes your Ka twin energy body. Just like filling the petrol tank in your car this fills up your outer outlining body with charges of electromagnetic light. **Those in the Ether World can connect with this charge since this is your own personal generator doing its thing.**

Sam: Like a generator providing electricity for your house?

Oh yes to create a spiralling magnetic energy field which spins right around you, oscillating to and fro like a spin dryer though, sometimes, bumps happen on contact with our world.

Sam: Bumps?

Because the energy of the material world moves at slow low frequencies compared to the Ether`s fast magnetic charge, the energy has to change frequency as it moves from one world to the other, then bumps happen and spontaneous effects burst into our world. **Now the invisible becomes visible.**

And this can happen anywhere, in anything since every single object has both an electric and a magnetic field. Electromagnetic currents charge about in the Ether.

Our ether friends use this charge to create spontaneous bursts of light into and through our world by means of sound and light vibrations by **WILLING this to happen.**

Sam: Can you tell me more about vibrations?

Vibrations oscillate from side to side as movement of energy.

The Ether is a world of vibrations which oscillate, zip in and out and travel across the dimensions. A person dies and then they become a fast moving vibration in the Ether world.

Actions and movements of energy have vibratory frequency.

Movement in our world happens through energy vibrations

Energy vibrates.......electrical charges fire.......energy sparks and releases out into the air and atmosphere.

Light vibrates in zig zag patterns as a great universal vibration. Waves of light are electromagnetic radiation.

Sam: But how does this make objects move?

Those in the Ether will the light to move.......... an electromagnetic light charge fires......this interacts with the vibrations of one specific object.

Atoms in the object are ninety nine percent space or ether, therefore it is ether substance itself which is moving.

Love flows at a high fast vibration beyond the speed of light.

They use love and light from the Ether World to generate an electro magnetic reaction where they want it to go.

THEY MOVE LIGHT TO PROVE THEY STILL EXIST.

Sam: Is every light outline electro magnetically charged?

Yes, light is focused......... a magnetic reaction flares out .... and is felt through an object or our own force field.

Sam: Okay is there something more scientific to tell me?

When an electromagnetic wave hits an atom, this is then absorbed and electrons are excited to a higher energy state. Now the object begins to move, the wave is then re emitted as electrons fall to a lower state.

Sam: In plain English the object is being magnetised?

Yes but the reaction won`t last. An electron, never stable in this excited state, has to move quickly to a lower state. The energy is then lost and the paranormal phenomenon has to end.
For Jurgen, all kinds of spontaneous things happened with objects in his house just after his nephew, Claus, had died. Claus was only eleven years old and something of a mischief maker, and he had stayed in Jurgen`s house for a six month period just three weeks before he was killed outright in a car.
Some of his things were still in the room he had stayed in with Jurgen, and one jar or container with a screw top was still there because nobody could ever open it. On one particular day, a week after Claus had died, Jurgen found this jar and gave the lid a quick twist. `Suddenly I found it opened easily and at exactly that same moment, the clock on the mantlepiece which had never worked, began ticking and it has worked ever since. It was Claus giving me some message that he was still around and still had energy to do this.

Also there was a very old painting on the wall of the landing showing an old man and woman and Claus had always said he didn`t like the picture because it was too dark.

On the next day I was looking at this painting and it began to glow with this unearthly light, like a halo, around the head of both the old man and the old woman.

There was no sun at all outside which could have been shining on the picture, and this glow only lasted for a very short time but it was definitely there. `

Through the area of the heart radiant waves of electromagnetic energy are sixty percent greater than in the brain. Love or hate is more effective than conscious mind thoughts. Waves of electromagnetic energy are 60% greater at the heart than the brain.

Ether space, all round us, is alive with interactions from each world. All of us are energy generators between the worlds.

Sam: Can you explain how magnetic energy works?

Waves need water to move......light needs ether to move.

The electromagnetic wave form moves energy in our universe by using the law of attraction. Electric and magnetic fields exist as pressure, tension and motion in the etheric world.

This pressure, tension and motion affects us all the time in various ways since we`re surrounded by electromagnetic light.

Sam: Is this how you feel the touch of someone who`s died

Yes manipulating light waves through the Ether causes a pressure in ether energy. An electromagnetic charge generates between the worlds.........now you feel the touch of somebody or a light pressure through your outer twin.

A magnetic force can attract, repulse or cause rotation and movement in magnetic fields.

Faraday, the scientist, discovered the magnetic field in the Ether which causes iron filings to be drawn towards a magnet all through the law of attraction. **Using intention, magnetism and attraction makes objects move**

Sam: Are electromagnetic waves the same as radio waves?

Yes, there is a type of electromagnetic wave with wavelengths greater than visible light, and these provide radio waves.

These fields, through the Ether, can`t be touched, like matter, but they do form part of the fabric of this world. Radio and TV signals flow at high, fast frequencies although the substance of the Ether vibrates at a still faster finer frequency.

Sam: Has anyone in history worked with magnetism?

Anton Mesmer did cure people with magnets and magnetic energy by drawing etheric energies in from just beyond the body to bring balance between the ether and physical body.

He claimed that the magnetic law of attraction and the power of ether not only keeps the sun moon and planets in place, in space but anyone could draw in this power to heal themselves.

He confirmed that every object has its own share of magnetic fluid which can be magnetised from other energy levels.

Electromagnetism can be hard to come to grips with, even though every one of us is surrounded by fields of this energy. So, once we`ve experienced electromagnetism in action, through other peoples` experiences, we will be ready to move on to the world of light.............

The pioneers of radio and TV including Marconi, Edison, Sir Oliver Lodge, Sir William Crookes and John Logie Baird all believed that spirit communication was possible and the first voice was recorded in 1860.

Chapter Thirteen

Electromagnetism in action

On the anniversary of Robert`s death, his friend Matt noticed the church clock had stopped at exactly the time he had died.

But Matt was ready for the unexpected because at Rob`s funeral he had already seen his old friend appear, dressed in a strange cloak and what looked like a kilt, dancing all around his grave shouting out about how free he was now. Rob was really back to being his cheeky old self in the way he had been before his illness.

Yet it had been hard work getting to and through the funeral because Matt`s car broke down and he had to take a taxi. Then, when the service was in process, all the lights in the church went out and extra candles brought in because nobody could get those lights working again.

And exactly the same thing happened back at the house where everyone was invited along to toast Rob`s health. Matt raised his glass for the toast, in the semi darkness of the late winter`s afternoon, and his glass broke in his hand at the moment he mentioned Rob`s name. It was at this very second that there was a loud bang and all the lights and power in the house failed completely. On searching for the trip switches, with a torch, every switch was in the right position and after five minutes all the power just came back on naturally.

After her husband had died following a prolonged illness, Joy says: `I walked out of his study and the door slammed shut as if to say he had gone. Then all the electrics in the house went out, at the same moment our son`s car conked out as he was coming to see me and, even as he tried to restart the car, there was a strong smell of his father`s cigars filling the air. `

A while after her husband had died, Fiona gave a girl a lift to the station and they were waiting in the car till her train came.

`My daughter rang on my mobile, ` Fiona says, `but the ring tone wasn`t one of mine..it was a jokey one that her father had on his mobile.......a sort of mock Indian voice of a man in a call centre going: `hello, hello,` so the ring tone was not one of mine but was definitely my husband`s. This shows me they still have a sense of humour where they are now. `

Barbara`s husband, Brian, died and she was dreading her birthday which is at the end of November. She told me: `At 5pm on the appointed day there was a ring at the doorbell and, since it was pitch dark outside, I was apprehensive about opening the door as my house is a bit remote. But I thought it might be my neighbour so I opened the door, having put the porch light on and there was nobody there.

Very strangely I do have security lighting that always comes on when anyone walks up the drive but this had not been triggered either, and everywhere around was in darkness. But instead of being scared I decided that this was Brian`s special way of wishing me a happy birthday.

And just to reinforce the message that this was Brian trying to contact me, the same thing happened twice more on that night, and there was nobody there when I opened the door and there was no wind, the night was still but I was not afraid at all.

All the lights went out in Highclere castle at the time of the death of Lord Caernarvon who discovered Tutankhamun`s tomb, and his dog let out an unearthly howl.

Marion`s husband died and he had always done everything around the home for her and taken care of her so that she found she had completely lost her confidence in her own abilities when she was suddenly alone. `I always left everything up to him, ` she said, `and had no idea how to do half the things that needed doing around the place.

Anyway, I wasn`t so young any more and just felt like I had been set completely adrift in a sea of fear and there was one thing that was really worrying me. I know it sounds silly now but I was scared of the fish pond. It had to be relined and I realised it needed doing about one month after Arthur had died.

So I stood there and wondered where on earth to start? I didnt have enough money to get someone in to help so it had to all be down to me but where would I start? I just stood there crying, feeling completely inadequate as you do when your loved one dies and leaves you. But then I began to realise I could hear his voice. It was in my head, Arthur`s voice and he was telling me very slowly and carefully that I could do it and that he would help me.

I rushed inside to get a notepad to write everything down to remember it but when I came back out the pen wouldn`t work. `Don`t worry, love, I`ll guide you all along the way,` he was telling me. And it felt so comforting, I can`t tell you, just to know he was around. Then he began to tell me which tool I needed and, somehow, it was as though he moved that specific tool forward to the front of the shed, each time, and I could find it without having to go rummaging through.

In the end it took hardly any time at all to do this fishpond which I had been resenting so much up till this time although I ended up being very grateful to it because the fishpond brought my Arthur back to me. `

Amanda was kicking herself because she had lost a very precious letter which her husband, Julian, had written to her after their first meeting. It was just two months after Julian`s death ~ which came completely out of the blue when he died in a car accident ~ when she went to a medium hoping they would be able to tell her where the letter could be. But she was disappointed to simply be told that Julian was going to help her find that letter again. Yet she couldn`t see how he could possibly help now that he was no longer physically with her.

Yet just one week later, she woke up from a very deep sleep

hearing Julian`s voice. He was telling her to go to the wardrobe and on the second shelf on the left she would find the precious letter. **He was right! The letter was there but Amanda knew, without any doubt whatsoever, that she would never have placed the letter in the wardrobe. So obviously Julian had put it there for her to find.**

Warnings from the after life

Warnings come from the other side about things that are about to happen for those loved ones left behind who are open enough to hear and heed these warnings.

Bill told me: `My wife, Muriel, died and I was off work for a while but I had to go back. I always took the bus to work, this was my routine, but there was one day when Muriel`s voice seemed to be telling me not to take the bus the next morning.

"What are you on about, woman?" I asked her. "I always take the bus, how else can I get to work for heaven`s sake?"

I didn`t really believe it could be her. And yet it can`t have been wishful thinking because why would I want her to come to me and tell me something like that?

I was going to ignore her advice and take the bus as usual but it just so happened that on this particular day I overslept. I never overslept, I don`t know what happened to me but I missed the bus.

And then when I did get to work, eventually, on a later bus, they had the local radio on and they gave out this message about the bus crash. That same bus, the one I was meant to be on, it crashed into a lorry at the traffic lights, and I found out later that the people who were hurt were sitting on the left hand side, half way back, exactly where I would always sit.

So I believed in her from then on, Muriel had told me true and now I listen to what she has to tell me. `

Jodie had not long passed her test and felt very brave driving along on her own in the car. But she suddenly felt she was not on her own. It was as though her mother ~ who died a year before ~ was with her, and that her mother asked her to drive a different way home on one particular night, as there was an obstruction on the road. Jodie went the other way and later learned the bridge had fallen down, and had she been on her former route she would have been directly beneath it and certainly crushed.

Animal connection from the Ether World

Rodney tells how his mother had always been in contact with people in the after world which slightly unnerved him. So when the time came for her to die he was wary as to how she would appear to, or in front of him.

Nothing happened the first night after she died but then, he tells me, ` On the second night suddenly and out of the blue I could feel her presence right behind me, although I never did see her, but she gave me a great hug which almost took my breath away. This left me feeling overwhelmed with immense feelings of so much love and this was so comforting and released my sense of fear. `

Two years later Rodney found himself the proud or not so proud owner of two Cavalier King Charles spaniel puppies with which he found it impossible to cope. He had only taken them on, originally, because he couldn`t say no to a friend, but they were very out of control, driving him mad and he knew he had to do something.

He was due to visit a medium, on one particular Sunday, to receive messages from his mother who had, before he acquired the puppies, told him from spirit to definitely not get another dog after his last one died. He had ignored that message to his cost, and on this Sunday, he says, ` the message came from my mother that she had it all in hand and was sorting the situation out for me. `

`So she knows this is the problem which right now is

uppermost in my mind? ` Rodney suggested to the medium and she confirmed: `Oh your mother knows, she is always with you in spirit, even in the car driving here, so I hope you were not speeding? `

The Monday came and he had no idea what was going to happen next, but he went up to a particular cafe which he sometimes visited, although never on a Monday.

He was talking to the lady serving at the counter and she said: `Oh you must see my brother, he`d love to take the dogs off your hands and give them a good home. `

`Okay, right,` Rodney responded feeling a bit overwhelmed at the speed with which everything was moving. His mother really did seem to have taken over, she still seemed to be sorting everything out for him despite having died a while before.

To add to the seeming coincidence, the lady at the counter said: `It just so happens that my brother is here now, today, over by the roses although he never normally comes in here on a Monday. It must be your lucky day. `

`Well I knew, ` says Rodney, `that this was not just my lucky day but also my mother stepping in and helping me out. I went over and talked to the brother and soon a deal was struck. The puppies had a new home with someone who could cope with their over exuberant energy.

I knew that I had my mother to thank for sending me to the nursery so that I could find a safe home for the dogs.

I had advertised, previously, but with no joy so this turned out to be the best deal all round for everybody, including the puppies. `

On the day I saw Rodney, at the clinic where I worked, he had just had his blood pressure tested and this was a bit on the high side so he came along for the doctor to advise him as to what he should do about it. `I wouldn`t have checked

or made the appointment had my aunt ~ who has also died ~ advised me that I needed to have it checked out as soon as I could. She said I needed to take something to bring my blood pressure down. ` And this he duly did.

His mother, whilst she was still alive, often saw people who had recently died standing at the foot of her bed, even and including her own mother. Rodney now finds he can often sense both the presence of his mother, and his grandmother, which sometimes leaves him unsure about which one is contacting him. He just feels a presence and hears a message in his head. Or sometimes the presence of one or other of his dogs decides to make itself felt.

`After my dog Emma died, I could hear the noise of her feet walking across the bedroom floor, and then the mattress went down on one side as though she had climbed on the bed and was sitting next to me.

I don`t consider myself particularly psychic, but there are times when my hands just go dead and my mother has told me that this is the spirit energy holding my hand.

Sometimes I have a similar slightly numb or cold feeling around my head and a vivid picture of my grandmother`s face comes through which brings me so much warmth

But there was one time, during an asthma attack, when I was really struggling for breath. In that moment I felt the light trace of fingers up the right hand side of my face and across the crown of my head. This had to be my mother sending me healing energy to make me sleep ~ which I did, instantly. When I woke the next day the asthma had gone. `

Rodney met up with his slightly psychic friend Jim, in Sainsbury`s, and Jim was standing by the checkout when he first saw him. Rod did all his shopping and was surprised to see Jim still standing in exactly the same place

as before, right by the same checkout, wearing a confused shocked look on his face. `Are you okay? Have you finished your shopping? `Rodney asked wondering why his friend had not moved on.

`No, I`m a bit worried because I watched you walking around the store and I`m sure Sainsbury`s have a `no dogs` policy. But there was this brown dog following you wherever you walked. `

`Oh that would be Emma, but don`t worry she`s not actually physically here, she died over a year ago,` Rodney told him.

Rodney is a kind and empathetic man who might not consider himself to be particularly intuitive or psychic, but when even slightly out of the ordinary events appear in our lives, spontaneously, they are designed to show us that those who now exist as etherics are still able to be in touch with us.

Chapter Fourteen

Into the Spirit World with NIGEL

Nigel is a medium who prefers to work from the stage rather than to undertake individual private sittings nowadays. He has a wonderful quirky humorous way of interrelating between the spirit world, and those who are so grateful and relieved to receive the messages he brings through to them, from their deceased loved ones.

In fact Nigel says he has never met a spirit ~ and he`s met a good few in his time having been in contact with spirit energy ever since he was a child ~ who wasn`t happy in the place where they now find themselves ie the spirit world.

He describes the spirit world as consisting of layers and layers of energy although it is never permitted for any of us here, in our earthly incarnation, to see the spirit world. He believes we are all spirit beings, in life, and of course beyond, and that in our life we will be in a certain level of spirit, and we will move on to a specific layer or spirit level when we depart from the physical world.

He started early to be aware of the presence of spirit energies, and when phone calls came through to his parents` house, telling that one or another relation had died, he knew all about the message that was about to be given before anyone answered the phone. He could tell them just who had died.

Nigel also has an amazing photograph of himself, aged about five or six, which shows a pillar of light behind at the same time as shining right through him, obviously intending to be an influencing presence in his life.

The greatest message of comfort which Nigel Gaff brings is that `nobody here walks alone,` and he tells me. `As a very young child we can all see spirit and we try to explain this to our parents but are immediately told that this is our: imaginary friend. Children will sit staring into nothing for long periods of time and sometimes you can see them connecting with or relating to someone else`s energy.

As a child all the chakras are open but the chakric centres which connect us to our energy body close down when we are about six years old, as the soul becomes grounded in the body and no longer the free spirit which it was before birth. Yet it will be again after death of the physical body.

So that we all become aware only of the three dimensional world from that time onwards, unless or until something jolts our awareness such as a near death or other psychic experience.

Where there are three parts to ourselves, two exist here and one doesn`t but continues to exist in the spirit world. `

I ask him about his guides and he begins by telling me: `One day when I was sitting here ` ~ we`re in the conservatory of his lovely house ~ `I looked out of the window and saw a Zulu warrior guide looking straight back at me and smiling. `

`How did he look? ` I ask

`Looking at those in spirit is like looking at an X ray and I can see the lines on the face but it is like they are there and yet not there. This is the best way I can describe this. And as soon as I looked away he had gone.

But, ` he wants to assure me, `we all have several guides who come in at different times in our lives as the soul continues to grow and experience what it needs to experience in life. Yet the guides come in to help just when they are needed.

In fact, ` he tells me, `there is a whole team of those in spirit energy who are lining up to support every one of us. We really are never alone, and they give us help and guidance when needed to send us in this or that direction, or to help us bump into the one person we need to meet at a specific time in life.`

Nigel has had some very vivid experiences whilst undertaking his mediumship role from the stage. On one particular evening he was looking to get a link in the audience to connect with the spirit energy he was sensing when he suddenly felt a pain in the side of his head. He found himself drawn to a woman in the front row and told her: ` I have a gentleman here and he was shot in the head in the trenches, and he has a message for you. `

`Oh that would be my grandfather, ` she responded quickly.

`Well I am getting a very vivid picture here of what was happening in those trenches that he is giving me. I can see his body falling down and all these other bodies falling down. I can hear the gunfire and smell the smoke and your grandfather is telling me that he just couldn`t make his body do anything any more, but that would be because he had died by that stage.`

Nigel could then continue to describe all kinds of things about her grandfather which reassured and convinced her that it was definitely this same grandfather who was coming through.

`Mediumship is dependent on how the medium feels, and if he is in a mood where he is less than his best then the images might not be so clear, or the links could be more unstable.

The soul,` he tells me, `is massive and like a hard drive on the computer because it is filled with limitless information about the person. When you go over you take all your memories and all the information with you. ` He tells that the `soul is the you that has been sent with a full set of instructions about the coming life. The soul works through the subconscious for such vital functions as the survival of the body, and also the life works you will do during your lifetime........ works that are already written down.

You choose your parents and the place you will live before you come in, and your soul is always protected in a spirit shape and form which could be thousands of years old except that there is no such thing as time or space in the spirit world.

In life the soul is always asking `why` and humankind is

always looking. Realising that Jesus came in as the son of God energy and that we murdered him and yet we are all this son of God energy.

What the soul seeks is how to expand and grow closer to the God energy in spirit, to climb those layers of energy in spirit always aiming in life, and in the spirit world, to get closer to the level and layer of the God energy. `

Nigel tells that `Once the body is finished spirit steps away and, at the point of death, fear leaves and the person is not alone in death any more than they are ever alone in life. **But at this point, as the chakras burst open, they release their energy to become wholly spirit energy and then vision comes through for the person who is leaving.**

The brain housing the mind dies and suddenly stops existing as the conscious mind also fades, but all the experiences of that life are already `on the system` and have recorded all of your life`s work. And as you go back home, you can have a look at the file of all you have done during the just passed life.

Then there is the process of the balancing of the soul in the form of karma so that people receive back from that which they themselves have handed out, in like measure. `

I ask him about the type of information he can give to those who come to see and hear him in a state of grief. He says that: `Sometimes it is not as graphic as, for instance, when I was in the trenches with the grandfather of the woman in the audience.` But the spirits provide him with the various evidences of how they passed, they give names, dates and other information which would be important to the person left behind such as holidays taken together or road names.

One time there was a young guy who came through when Nigel was on stage with about two hundred and fifty people, all watching and waiting expectantly. `As he came through I felt the impact to my own head that this young guy had felt as his car had skidded and hit a tree. I looked around in the audience and found his friend who had not been a great believer in anybody`s mediumship abilities. I could tell him the message I was receiving that, on his way to the hall, all he had asked of the evening and all that was about to take place was: **`I want my friend to come through to tell me he is allright. `**

Sure enough the young man in the audience confirmed that this was exactly what he had been thinking on his way in.

`Well your friend wants me to tell you that he knows you`re off to Australia shortly, and that he is coming with you. He`s telling me all about the car that he crashed and how it was a bit flashy and had all the extra lights on it and everything. But also that he was a bit reckless and shouldn`t have driven it that way, though he is all right, he is fine. `

Once having passed on the message to the young man who was shortly to go to Australia, this guy had no choice but to believe in what he had been told. He knew it was his friend coming through. On another occasion there was a young woman who had recently had a miscarriage and Nigel could tell her: `You had a name for the baby and after she had died you wrote her a letter and buried it in the garden. `

`How did you know that? ` The woman asked, `I never told anyone that, not anyone!`

And still, in his role as a medium, Nigel must continue with his survival evidence because he is helping so many people.

Where he is asked the question about why or how children can die when so young he confirms that they: `Were only meant to touch the earth plane for a brief period but that they will stay around in spirit, with their parents till they are adults. They will continue to be part of the family unit, as though living that life, just growing on a different, metaphysical level. They will still be there for all the christmasses and anniversaries, Easter and birthdays, they will still be around.

He explains that: `young kids can be quite mischievous when in spirit, and can move things around like keys or pictures or affect the electrical gadgets of the house, or turn on and off the light switches, even change the TV channel if they so choose.

`I was basically a decorator as my trade and I went to a house with a colleague who worked for me, and this was the house of a lonely lady with a daughter. My mate and I were in the bedroom, and it was a lovely warm day, but suddenly we were both aware that there was a very cold energy over the bed.

I knew that this was connected with her son who had died in a motorbike accident. Her grief had been so great that she`d held on to him, held on to his energy here in that bedroom. I had to make her aware of what was happening and I was able to release him and he could then go back to where he was meant to be, in the spirit world.

When I was stripping the wallpaper, there was a picture which emerged behind on the wall. This was crudely drawn as would be the case of a child`s drawing. It was a picture of a square house with four windows and the front door as you see children draw. There was, though, a line in grey going up from the house and it came to a halt as though it was broken off. And the spirit of her son told me that he had drawn this line through the wallpaper covering, only couldn`t go any further or continue the line any further up because he was still trapped in the physical world and wanted to go home and be free.

I knew that it was no coincidence that the person who would come to decorate the house should be myself with my clairvoyant abilities so that I was able to set this boy`s spirit free. There used to be, ` Nigel tells me, `what were described as rescue circles in the old days to set people free and there would be fields of people who needed rescuing in this way.

In the spirit world the soul never rests but exists, ` Nigel believes `as a pillar of energy with the same qualities that the person had in life.

I was aware, one time, of a woman in the audience whose husband had really loved Frank Sinatra, and I could tell her that he had met up with Frank in the spirit world.

I have also myself met up with Barry Sheene in the spirit world, and Liberace often comes through playing his piano and smiling so cheerfully. The Cray twins came through one time when there was a woman in the front row where the spirit of her uncle appeared. He described himself as having been a `bad man`. He said he had been a friend of the Crays and knew them and I could hear the echo of a voice in the background saying: `You can run but you can`t hide, ` and this was the voice of one of the Cray twins.

Not long after I had started as a medium I was giving the evidence to the audience, and the medium secretary said that Kenneth Williams was around and working with me. Then at another church, another time, that medium secretary said Kenneth William`s energy was around and liked working with me. But the thing is I like to keep the atmosphere light and humorous, it is so much easier for the spirit energy to come through when people are happy or laughing. They just can`t get through when there is too much negativity or people are weighed down in self pity with their grief. And people like Kenneth Williams help raise the vibration because of all the laughter they are able to engender.

I had Sid James in this room, ` Nigel tells me about another occasion, `there were a few people and we had met as a circle and I was sitting back in my chair and relaxing and meditating when, all of a sudden, the people around me started to say that they could see Sid James` face superimposed over mine. Sometimes it happens like that and the spirit energy superimposes itself over your features, but this definitely helped a colleague of mine in the room to believe in spirit.

Mediums are born and it is not something you learn, ` Nigel says. `Whilst everybody is psychic most people don`t use this ability, not everyone is a medium by any means. Although there are those who think they are and this can lead to mediumship of the wrong kind of which I`m always very wary. You don`t want to build peoples` hopes up falsely. I like to stand on stage and allow the spirit connections to come to me and am not looking for the commercial side of being a medium.

But whilst I do bring a lot of people through I want to make people laugh and raise the vibration to help even more come through. Any negative energy can so easily block spirit.

True mediums want to help, as do the spirits who appear to reassure their relatives. **We are all always connected to the spirit world by an etheric thread or cord,** and we will all die one day so wherever our loved ones have gone so we will go to, to the spirit world.

Sometimes with me, when I am working at places like the new centre at Hookwood, people who don`t normally come through do so with their messages. But there are spirits of loved or not so loved ones that people don`t want to hear from.

Sometimes someone will come through to those they have left behind who didn`t like them in life. One time there was a woman at the back and there was this very large man who came through in connection with her. He wore a big belt, his name was Jim and he had the smell of alcohol around him so was obviously a heavy drinker in life ~ spirits gather around them the energies of how they were when they were alive so that their relatives can recognise them ~ and this woman, at the back, was very reluctant to have anything to do with him.

`No, I hated him when he was alive,` she said, `he was a mean bastard and I don`t want to hear from him. ` However, mediums have to go with what they are given and she had to recognise his energy being present because there is always a reason for spirits to come through. He was there for a reason and had a message to give, and this guy was obviously very sorry for how he had been in life and how he acted towards her.

My own Dad would come in sometimes and help me, especially when there were happenings which had taken place during the war when he had been there, and he could help me realise exactly what was happening.

We have supreme intelligence through our soul, but when we come in and are born the memory system is wiped and we have to start again in each lifetime.

But there are those who, no matter how much evidence they are shown, can never believe in what we, as mediums, do and they won`t or can`t let themselves believe that there is any more than just this life. They feel that when it ends, it ends, despite all the evidence we can provide to show this is not so.

Simon is a friend of mine, in Horsham, but he swore he wouldn`t come along and see me work. For some reason he did turn up, on one night, when I was at the Black Dog in Crawley, and he was shaking with fear at what might happen, he couldn`t allow himself to believe in any of it. He stood at the bar and tried to ignore us but there was a woman whose father had died of emphysema.

The father`s name was John, and I was giving all the evidence about how he died and how his lungs filled up with fluid and he just couldn`t breathe any more, how he liked snooker and played for money. I gave this woman all the evidence she needed to know it was her father, could tell her just how much he had loved her, and that he loves her still. She was emphatic it was him, John her beloved father.

Yet Simon couldn`t allow himself to believe in even such evidence as this, he just walked off and walked away still refusing to believe. It is never the medium`s job to say this is how it is, mediums are guided all the time by the same spirit energies that everyone has but few realise this, and the medium does not know what is going to happen or where spirit is going to take them. `

I ask Nigel about reincarnation and he tells me that with one notable famous exception most mediums do believe that we come back again to experience another lifetime and then another. And then he begins to tell me about a previous lifetime of his own: `It was when I was living in Ifield and I was sitting in my office to the side of the house when I looked out of the window and saw a teacher in the old fashioned gowns they used to wear ~ and probably still do ~ at Eton.

And a few years later my wife`s friend died of breast cancer and when we were at the funeral, again in Ifield, I looked down and found that I, too, was wearing the same sort of long black gown or tunic that they wore in Eton. I could hear a choir singing around me and could suddenly see many schoolboys all dressed in similar apparel.

Later on I went back home and looked up Eton School on the website and you could follow your way right around the school`s buildings. I was following this corridor around when I said to my wife that when we went round the next corner there would be a big plaque on the wall. We scrolled down and sure enough it was there.

I am pretty sure that I was at school at Eton, in that lifetime, and led a very comfortable existence.

As I said before the memories and interests that we carry from this life, and our previous lifetimes, are all stored in the subconscious mind or our soul, it is just that we are very seldom able to access them in this current life.

But I guess that the most important message I can give for we who still inhabit a physical body is that our spirit always wants each of us to get the most out of life. We are never alone as we walk through this life, not one of us and there is always some spirit guide around you twenty four hours a day. Or behind you, in teams, making sure you will meet those you are meant to meet. And if you are not walking down the right road then they will come in to make the adjustments.

Of course we all have free will but we are also being helped, all of the time. What is important for your soul is how you live and not how you die.

Sometimes when I am just sitting relaxing in the room I am aware of a sparkle or a pillar of light beside me, for a few seconds, and then it just goes. But I know the spirit energy is all around us, helping us and I say again that I have never met a spirit who was not happy with where they are now. `

There are times when Nigel Gaff, from Crawley, becomes disheartened by the commercial need for the world to follow the wrong tack and try to make money from the spirit world connection. However, Nigel is on a path of truth which brings great comfort, and belief, to so many people which reasssures them about how their loved ones continue to exist, in spirit, after their physical death. Therefore he cannot give up in his connection to the spirit world.

He describes autistic children as having an extra dimension or gift in that they have a closer connection, than the rest of us, to their subconscious mind, or soul wisdom.

Nigel does have inspirational knowledge, and the spirit world seems to have no intention of ever allowing him to retire from his innate gift of knowing. He is bound to continue to act as the medium or connection to the incredible world which exists just beyond the normal conscious awareness of everybody.

Messages of importance

`Oh Paul I`ve lost my engagement ring, ` Marcia cried out, it was only a matter of ten days since Paul had died and she desperately wanted to wear the ring for the funeral.

She was so upset about losing this vital ring as something to connect her to him, and turned the whole house upside down as she searched for it. But later, as it was growing dark, she sat down in a chair in a heap of exhaustion and could swear that she heard Paul`s voice telling her to look behind the clock.

`Don`t be silly, why would my ring be behind the clock? ` She asked him but, looking at the clock, she was aware that there was something very odd about it. It was ticking oddly.

`It was a weird sound, ` she said, `sort of haphazard and irregular, so I went to investigate. And then I could see it was leaning to one side with something underneath one of the legs.

I hadn`t noticed this before, but there was this envelope under one leg. `What is that doing there? ` I asked myself and I opened it up and there in all its shining glory was not only my beautiful engagement ring, but also the copy of Paul`s will for which we had been searching everywhere.

I don`t know how he did this, but that envelope was definitely not there when we were turning the house upside down, looking for both the ring and the will. Yet it was through this irregular ticking of the clock that he managed to show me where to find both of them. `

Darren`s father, who was really missing his wife when she died, was fishing down at the lake and he said to her, `please come in and give me some sort of sign that you`re still around.` And she did, all of a sudden the alarms on both the two fishing rods went off and she had caught two fish, too, as part of the sign that she was there with him They all know she is around in the house because they can smell her `musk` perfume.

Duncan could hear a strange unexpected voice coming from the hall of his house. He walked up to the place where he felt the voice was coming from and seemed to walk right the way through the voice and to come out the other side. There seemed to be no definite source, the sound echoed all around him, but he felt the voice was urging him to do something ~ this was five days after his mother died ~ and it was a female voice. For some reason he felt the voice pushing him towards the front door which he then opened and found his mother`s precious cat sitting very quietly, drenched and looking very thin on the step outside, hardly able to mew or make contact.

This cat had disappeared immediately after his mother`s death and they had all been so busy they had virtually forgotten about it, but now his mother had given the message so that the cat could be rescued. Duncan set about taking care of it and bringing it back to health ~ for his mother`s sake.

Animals definitely tell us when loved ones who are no longer with us, physically, are nevertheless around in our energy field.

Dogs growl and bark when there is nobody obviously there, cats look scared and turn and run out of the room when faced with inexplicable movement in the energy and how can we tell what they`re seeing?

Jimmy`s dog, Sheppa, became even more of a loyal companion after his wife, Martha, died. One evening he pointed to a large photograph of Martha, `look Sheppa, your mum, where is she? ` He asked, feeling stupid, just needing to do something to amuse and haul himself out of the depths of his self pitying energy.

Sheppa did look at the photograph and then she looked at the chair where Martha had always sat, as her preference, and then Sheppa leapt up, wagging her tail, going first to the chair and then to the door in echo of the way Martha would get up from her chair and go to the door to take her for a walk. Did this dog have some kind of power of awareness or was it just that the dog was ultra intelligent, who can tell?

Flowers through the Ether world

Nature can also play its part in offering ways for us to be contacted from the after life. Mike had loved a rose he had seen, called `Julia`s rose`, and Dee bought it for Mike after he died and planted it in the garden. One week before what would have been his 70th party there were three buds, but they all just completely died by the time of that party, despite the bush being watered, since Mike never wanted that party to happen..

Mary found that after her sister died, there was an intense smell of lavender every time she went to bed and this had been her sister`s favourite smell and plant in the garden. The brother of the family also noticed the smell of the sister`s favourite perfume every Sunday which was her favourite day of the week.

Joan planted two of Derek`s favourite roses after he died and he came through a medium friend. `He said he wanted to thank me for those roses and that he would watch over them and make sure they lasted and flourished. And they did, they`re still flowering years later. ` Jill knew that her mother always loved red anaenomes and, after her mother died, she planted some around her garden, seeing her mother regularly.

`But then I had to move to a new house, ` she tells me, `and I was worried that my mother might not be with me so much in the new house. But soon after I moved in, in completely the wrong season for any flowers at all to be showing, especially anaenomes, I noticed one day that right beside the front door there was this red anaenome blooming brightly as proof that my mother`s energy was right there with me. `

Cathy`s sister died but on the very next day, on coming downstairs, Cath found her sitting room filled with white feathers, white rose petals and a beautiful feeling of peace.

Chapter Fifteen

LIGHT and NEUTRINOS

Sam: You say light is vital to the after life situation?

Light is everything, Sam, messages and contact can ONLY happen **by travelling through waves or particles of light.**

Ancient Egyptians believed they had to encourage the sun through twelve gates of the night to return on the next day.

The whole universe is affected by the nature of light. Light waves are travelling energy ~ as high frequency electromagnetic vibrations ~ always on the move, transmitting through the fabric of mysterious invisible ether.

Sam: So you have to have light waves for objects to move?

Oh yes. Light beams have to push against any object which gets in their way as they travel through the Ether.

An actual physical pressure creates in the light outline of any object in the path of light ....THE OBJECT MOVES!

The technical bit: light pressure is equal to the power of a light beam divided by the speed of light creating such tremendous power it can even accelerate the spin of asteroids.

Light waves are composed of electric and magnetic fields and light waves come in different frequencies and energies.

When light hits an object, various things could happen:

1. The light wave reflects and is scattered out *from* the object.
2. The wave is absorbed *by* the object and changes direction
3. The light wave passes *through* and has no effect at all.

Any one or all of these actions happen at one and the same time. So imagine you are going ten pin bowling and only three pins are left standing. The first time you throw a ball of light you hit just one pin......... light sparks out in waves from that pin......... and the pin falls over.

The next time you throw your light ball you hit just one other pin, the light waves ~ heading in a northerly direction ~ are absorbed by that pin. Now they have to turn around and shoot out in a westerly direction, leaving the pin wobbling.

The last time you throw your ball light waves pass straight through and leave the pin standing where it was with absolutely no effect whatsoever.

Light is nature`s way of transferring energy through space which can make objects move.

Also as light moves through a material the motion of light waves interact and slow .....visibility increases.....***suddenly something appears!*** *Let`s look at* atoms and photons next.

Sam: I`ve heard of atoms but what are photons then?

Okay, Sam, the universe is made of matter and energy.

All physical things around you, that pen or the table, are made from particles which called atoms, as well as molecules.

Atoms are particles and elements and they can`t be broken down any more. Matter has 4 states: solid, liquid, gas, plasma.

Think of something solid like ice and you`ll find all the molecules packed in tightly together in your chunk of ice. The molecules can`t move much, and then only slowly

Add heat, the molecules separate to form a liquid...... water.

Now boil the water, molecules move and try not to interact.

Sam: This is when it becomes steam ~ yes?

Yes it is and atoms are now in a gas state. The only difference between the states is the amount of energy added to matter.

Energy makes changes happen, crucially, light is energy!

Potential energy is stored ready to use. Kinetic energy is in use

Add light... energy changes from potential to kinetic state

Sam: So this helps our etheric friends make things move by using beams of light to add energy to matter?

Yes, Sam, you`ve got it. So now let`s look in on photons:

A photon is a bundle of electromagnetic or light energy.

Photons are light force carriers which strike an object and transfer their momentum through to that specific object.

See light as a collection of one or more photons travelling in electro magnetic waves ~ created from zillions of photons

Photons are produced by the light source through an object.

Atoms in matter bind together to make molecules of a substance which has electrons.......now photons of light contact and connect with these electrons............. light is absorbed......a luminescent appearance of light shines out through the Ether

Some substances create glowing phosphorescence having been subjected to a bath of light for a certain length of time.

Sam: This is like what happened with the Baron when he was saturating all those objects with sun or moonlight isn`t it?

The Baron and his team saw natural phosphorescence from objects appearing through an otherworld eerie light.

An electron in an atom, inside an object, absorbs the energy of a photon of light which it sends back out the way it came in.

The angle of a beam of light can be altered by a magnetic field. ***When the Baron had subjected objects to moon or sunlight, rays of light would shine and radiate out in different directions to prove the universal existence of the magni force.***

Light can be seen by the human eye as a magnetic radiation. A beam of light shines in different dimensions.....light wavelengths change........yet the frequency remains constant.

Light rays are streams of high velocity atoms. Motion is the movement of physical atoms. The Ether is filled with zillions of charged light particles creating light movement everywhere.

*Sam: I`**ve** seen flashes of light is this connected with Dad?*

Well spotted, Sam, and probably loads of people do vaguely notice short sharp flashes of light scurrying past them after someone has died, but they put it down to seeing things.

In fact this is very exciting because these are communications from the Ether world. What you see is the charged particles, zooming through the Ether. These are light messages from ether individuals trying to gain our attention. Virtual particles appear and disappear regularly as excited bursts of energy through every realm to exert an ether pressure.

The Ether always exerts a certain pressure on us which we never feel but it is possibly happening more than we think.

Maggie was trying to make her way through layers of grief. Mike`s death had come so out of the blue and all she wanted was just to be aware that he was around somewhere. `And then the most amazing thing happened, ` she said. `The first time it happened I ust put it down to being my imagination. No, it couldn`t have been him!

I felt this gentle kind of pressure on my right hand when I was sitting at my desk, holding my head down between my two hands. It was as though he was trying to lift my head up. And then there was another time when I was sure he touched my cheek, only I tried to convince myself that it was just the wind from the open window. The third time, though, there wasn`t any doubt in my mind that his two hands were on my shoulders. This was exactly what he used to do when he was going to massage my neck with first of all the hands on my shoulders as though asking permission to massage me. I knew then that this had to be Mike and when I heard about how those who had died could exert this pressure through the Ether energy, I knew absolutely that on every one of those three times it had been Mike. He is still here with me. `

Once a person has moved on to become wholly etheric their

sense of power increases and they find they can affect our energy fields, and material reality, to prove they are here.

This is what your father has been trying to do, Sam, it is a gradual process but he wants you to know he is part of the all seeing field and level of light energy. Light energy fields are not only all around him, but all around you too.

Now could be the time to look at neutrinos?

Sam: Okay what are neutrinos then?

To see the flashing light energy of neutrinos, think of supernovas where stars explode. **Each time this happens a great burst of light appears in the sky.**

Neutrinos are involved in this light outburst since they are created from thermonuclear reactions as radioactive elements of stars release in their dying process

Their last yet greatest moment fills the sky with brilliant light. Billions of neutrinos travel from sun across the cosmos.

They arrive and stream right the way through each of us and throughout our world, in every second of our lives. They prove just how insubstantial our world is.

We see ourselves and our objects as solid matter but neutrinos just pass right the way through it all, never even slowing their pace, or allowing themselves to be affected.

Sam: Can we see neutrinos?

Light travels through the Ether at the fastest speeds of all.

As light hits something transparent ~ like water ~ it slows yet neutrino particles do not. At this very second a cone of pale blue light releases, and this can be measured and seen.

A neutrino is a kind of elementary *ghost like* particle which can highlight anything. ***There have been a few times when I have seen my husband`s whole face in a kind of flashing light neutrino way as features outlined in white neutrino light.***

In 1956 neutrinos were found to be able to penetrate the thickness of lead, at the same time stretching their power up to the nearest star without hitting anything on the way. They have mass and interact gravitationally with other massive particles.

They are also the common denominators for particle reactions

Sam: Does this have anything to do with nuclear reactions?

Yes these reactions occur when cosmic rays hit atoms.

As a cosmic ray travels through matter, it will experience a process which is similar to what happens as light passes and shines through a transparent material.

All these neutrinos, across the universe, spend their time busily oscillating away, here and there, as they travel from the sun and stars down to earth. Their oscillating side to side movement varies with different light currents, but can create a flashing light effect. **When people see light flashes, or unexpected movements just beyond normal vision, these are active neutrinos oscillating through matter and space.**

And of course neutrinos exist in and through the Ether.

So with all these neutrinos blinking in and out of existence there`s always the chance of a flashing, sparking light appearing for you, from the fabric of the Ether.

Normally, however, neutrinos keep themselves hidden. You are lucky to have seen them.

Sam: But they need an extra charge to be visible to us?

Yes they need an extra magni force surge of power released from the other world.And these brilliant neutrinos are clever little things because they have this other ability, too, they can make the normally invisible Ether visible to the human eye.

This is just for a split second or two if someone is aware enough to understand what is happening. ***It took the Baron a while to realise what was happening by seeing flames of light.***

Sam: It sounds like we all need to keep our eyes open?

Yes it would be great to see the fast spinning spiralling ether magic shows ~ which continually happen in our world as bursts of flashing ether light ~ erupt through the air as those who have died REACH OUT FROM THE ETHER WORLD INTO OUR WORLD in a bid to help us.

The Friday night after Samantha`s husband died, and the week before his funeral where she felt all the light in her life had gone out, she sat quietly with only one lamp on in the house. `Suddenly, ` she says, `I realised the light in the passageway to the hall had switched itself on. I went to check and found all the lights, in every room of the house, had come on, the radio played and front porch light was on.

This had to be Jeff, telling me that he WAS still with me and that there WOULD still be light in my life. He proved he was here with the lights, which gave me comfort to get me through the funeral which I had been dreading.`

The universe is **all light anyway, death is merely a return.**

I have all kinds of experiences to relate later on, Sam, and as I mentioned I have had two or three occasions since Peter died where I have undergone some sort of strange sensation as though I, too, can feel what he felt on his last night.

There was one time when it was almost as though Peter was trying to reach through to me so strongly that I could see this silver blue light reflecting from my fingertips. But then I could feel migraine symptoms through my right temple and I had to ask him to stop throwing flashing neutrinos at me!

I have several times been through what I can only describe as transformative experiences with him since he died.

And several times he has been able to demonstrate to me how he is using the universal memories stored in the Akayshic Hall of Records to show a shape or form of energy. This is how he showed his fawn jacket to Debbie or his punk hair.

*T*he spirit goes on beyond shape or form, and continues to exist as a point of light. This point of light has an awareness which still relates to us and our own life story. It is this spirit shining through a level of light which mediums are able to see. **We live in a double world but mostly in the wrong one.** *Sam: Can you sum up for me how Dad makes things happen?*

There are certain necessary ingredients starting from:
Intention: The Ether World has a will and intention of energy. An electrical charge can erupt from their world to our own Through love and intention `etherics` manipulate light.

Magnetic Energy: Electrical charges cause a beam of light to flash, shine and erupt. Movements of magnetic electrical energy resonate with the fabric of the Ether.
Radiant Outline: The magni force power radiates through an object`s outline.........a radiant outburst of light erupts around the object, an outburst affects atoms and virtual particles inside the object ....and the object has to move.
Light Power and Pressure: Light beams push against the object standing in their path.........causing physical pressure which forces the object to move. Light energy forces the molecules in the atoms to travel at a faster frequency.
Light Waves and visibility: Ether individuals manipulate light ....light moves through a material and the object becomes more visible. The previously invisible appears.
Indents to show a presence: A particle of light creates a movement in the Ether........an indent or impression creates in the etheric levels.......an ether presence becomes visible in our level of reality or tangible as they touch our hand or face.
These are the messages given to me from the other side of life to explain appearances or the movement of objects and energy within our material world reality.

Chapter Sixteen

An alternative LEVEL OF HEALING

Sam: Can you now tell me more about healing using etheric energy? I guess that`s how it works?

We could begin with the realisation that every cell in the body contains enough genetic ~ etheric ~ information to create a clone or a duplicate of the body just like a hologram.

Sam: Is this how people who have lost a leg or an arm say, feel like its still there because of the aching?

Yes they feel this through their etheric energy double body which is like a hologram right the way round us.

The holographic effect in the whole of nature, round and through us and everything, happens in our double or energetic twin body`s electro magnetic fields. Acupuncture works on the holographic energy body, not the tangible physical body.

When you have such things as heart transplants ~ where the heart carries its own energy field containing all kinds of information about a person ~ this ether information is being transferred to someone else once the heart is transplanted.

Quite simply the body`s energy fields are incredibly powerful. They transmit ether energy and electricity through every cell in the physical body electro magnetically

The methods of treatment which come from the East are based on a belief in the vital energy which permeates the body. An acupuncturist aims to sedate or stimulate that energy depending upon whether it is deficient or excessive.

Acupuncture is based on the belief that chi flows around the body in channels. These channels are called meridians and they act as energetic etheric pathways.

There are twelve bilateral meridians, two central with one on the back and one on the front. Each meridian has a two hour period where the chi flows through more strongly.

According to Eastern theory man is the microcosm mirroring the universal macrocosm ~ to echo the physical and etheric world ~and everything has this duality. In nature the vital force of chi has two aspects of expression, Yin and Yang

The two balance each other yet ultimately one becomes the other ~ in the same way that the Ether world interpenetrates our material world.

Yin is the shady side of the hill and Yang is the sunny side.

Chi flows through the body along pathways where the subtle energy flow can be blocked. Acupuncture seeks to release specific points along the meridians, using needles to clear these blocks.

When it comes to the moving of energy in practices such as cranio osteopathy work ~ used by chiropractors and osteopaths ~ they work on the level where the etheric meets the physical. From here they move a fluid around the body to help the healing process.

Or you could say they are moving etheric energy, in fluid form, by gentle manipulation as they work at the base of the skull to relieve tension, and pain and bring the body back into harmony. In effect they bring balance between etheric and physical energies.

Membranes and fluid surround and support the brain and spinal cord and the fluid within the membranes continuously drains and refills. A practitioner of this etheric fluid movement can release the emotional and physical stresses on both the body and the head of a person.

We ourselves have an inner and outer etheric healer waiting to do this for us, all it takes is the addition of love and light which come from our etheric level to release our blocks.

Where spiritual healing takes place this healing again works on the spiritual etheric level of a person`s energy. The practitioner has the spirit wisdom to connect with and draw through the healing energies from the etheric world.

They sense the flowing movement within the patient`s body, not as strong as a vibration and not necessarily at the seat of the pain as indicated by the patient, but the spirit healer is aware of what is happening`

They believe they are working with and through the life force or the spirit light energy of the ether. They see themselves as acting as a channel who is invigorated by working with this energy as they tap into a person`s Ka outer ether body energy, and sometimes this can be done remotely.

Based on the premise that physical and mental health is dependent on the free flow of blood and energy ~ as Chi or Qi in Chinese belief ~ round and through the body, Chi Gung, Shiatsu massage and Tai Chi practice help free the blocked disrupted flow of subtle energy.

The practice of these techniques alters our connection with our ether outlining body.

Homeopathy has been around for over two hundred years and is a method of healing which helps the whole system. The homeopathic remedies resonate with the etheric body from the substance provided ~ where each remedy is diluted hundreds of times ~ to then work through the levels of a patient`s energy.

`The energy of a substance leaves an energetic imprint on or in the physical body ~ where something such as mercury can be having a negative effect ~ and it is only by using the same energy, in the form of homeopathy, that the energetic disturbance can be released and taken away, ` Anitra Harris, an inspired homeopath from Tunbridge Wells tells me.

`In the case of grief this will impact on your whole energy and being so that I would then suggest treatment through taking a remedy to match that grief you will be suffering as a supportive method of healing. ` ***I can personally confirm how homeopathy works as a method of energy healing, especially in my case where a specific homeopathic remedy for grief was sent to me by Anitra when I myself was first bereaved.***

Anitra tells me that `all matter is permeated with energy which can be liberated for the purpose of curing disease. The whole curative effect of homeopathy is not a material affair but is involved with what is termed `energy`. Since the remedy is "dynamic" and not material it follows that the level of disorder it works on belongs to the same, ` as given by Samuel Hahnemann. `

Anitra continues to describe what is perceived as the `vital force` through homeopathy ~ or as our investigation is discovering this to be the light charge of the ether body ~ as `proving its existence by the fact that when the disturbed organism (dis-ease) of a person is properly tuned with the administration of the correctly prescribed remedy, the person not only experiences the alleviation of his symptoms, but has the feeling of life harmoniously flowing through him. `

The vitalistic way of thinking believes this vital force connects the individual with the ultimate unity of the Universe,` Anitra says as is the case of ether flowing through our outer body and on universally. She describes how the Renaissance Alchemist Paracelsus reported `energy radiating from one person to another which could act at a distance, and he believed this energy could harmonise the body and restore health, or it could poison the body and cause disease. `

And then there is the practice of Reiki where, under Japanese practice, `Rei` means wisdom and divine knowledge, and `Ki` is the energy that surrounds and permeates everything ~ as another name for Ether energy. Reiki, therefore, is a particular energy frequency for healing purposes, and self healing, which works with the Ki energy at an increased vibration.

Where the Ki or ether energy is everywhere, flowing through everything all the time, Reiki specifically flows to and through those who have been specially attuned to a certain vibrational frequency. This attunement is able to be passed on through Reiki Masters, energetically, once they undertake the sacred ceremony for future practitioners.

Once again the belief is in how it is imperative to keep Ki or etheric energy flowing freely around and through the physical body. This is where Reiki as a healing art comes in.

During the attunement process for the Reiki practitioners ~ the energy clearing taking three weeks ~ Reiki energy flows into the physical and energy bodies so powerfully that specific parts of the auric/etheric field are cleared connected with the physical, emotional, mental and spiritual aspects of the self. After each level of attunement, the vibrationary rate at which the healer operates is raised from a normal rate of 250 cycles a second up to anything between 400 to 800 cycles a second.

The clearing happens through the chakras ~ the spinning wheels of energy which connect the physical to the etheric level ~ as the Reiki flows through to clear the blockages throughout the energy system.

An Interview with Margaret, Master Reiki and Spiritual Healer

Margaret is a lovely caring healing lady who tells me about how Reiki heals through from the aura or etheric body to the physical body in a way to increase the range and outreach of shimmering ether light force energy around a person.

And during her treatments of healing what she is doing is to bring the Reiki symbols down into the etheric level of the aura which surrounds a patient`s body. She always gives special attention to and concentration on the symbol for peace, as well as another symbol for harmony, so that all of her patients leave feeling balanced and calm.

Margaret explains how she follows the Reiki practice of bringing the power symbol down through her crown where the energy releases out down her arms and through her hands for the healing to be given. She also tells of the symbols for distant healing, as well as the healing of the past present and future which she uses through body mind and spirit. She explains how this sometimes results in her patients seeing themselves as they were in past times, in previous lives, in various costumes or clothing which applied at the time.

Having undertaken the sacred ceremonies of attunement ~ raising the vibratory rate of the four upper energy centres attuned to the etheric body ~ her conscious awareness and energy expand to bring healing energy for others to share.

She also teaches and attunes people in the different degrees of Reiki practice and tells me: `In one particular course there was a young woman being attuned who had a flat voice with no expression. She was lacking in confidence, in herself, especially when speaking out or in undertaking the meditations we were all experiencing. However, when I undertook the attunement associated with mental energies, through the throat and brow chakra, she suddenly started choking.

Once she managed to stop choking and speak again, she told me that she had always been told that nobody was in the least bit interested in anything she had to say. Therefore, she had learned to keep quiet and not speak up most of the time. But a week later, as the attunement was beginning to have an effect, her voice completely cleared and she could talk to others about all kinds of things she had never managed to discuss before. `

`What do people see when they are being treated with Reiki? I ask Margaret and she tells me they commonly see images of unicorns, colours, faces, people and past life flashes or beautiful sunsets and all kinds of uplifting light displays with the sky ablaze with primordial light. And some are able to see the world illuminated with that special light normally beyond the visible light spectrum, as they look through etheric layers.

`I had one particular patient, ` she says, `who came to me who had a more masculine than feminine appearance, and energy, and she saw faces and various past lives in different periods. In one life she could see vividly that she wore a helmet and armour, was very masculine in her stance with a deep throated voice.This could explain the look and feel of her energy in this present time.`

These visions into past life usually seem to have relevance with the present. Another patient saw an old crone type woman dealing in herbs to heal those around. This lady always had a particular interest in herbs herself, and now she could see why.

One particular young woman came to see Margaret and she was `Like a mirror which had had a stone thrown against it that had cracked the mirror into shards of glass, ` Margaret tells me. `By the end we put things back together again and managed to soothe and smoothe all the rough edges to her previous energy.

In other words Margaret`s gift of healing, through Reiki, had aligned the etheric body with the physical again. `Your hands lead you to areas that you don`t expect to follow to feel a disturbance in someone`s inner energy. You can feel this through their etheric outline, ` Margaret says, `and so much is held in the auric energy because illnesses appear in the auric/etheric outline before they appear in the physical.

But through Reiki we are able to send the energy where it is needed as the body wisdom takes over. Once we work with the chakras each one resonates with one of the endocrine glands, and the accent is always on the heart centre or chakra. `

The patient who appeared to be in a state of being like shards of broken glass had a husband who was very keen for her to attend her appointments with Margaret because he told his wife: `When you come back from Margaret that thing is always so big around you. `

`What thing, what do you mean? ` His wife asked in confusion.

`Oh you know that energy thing, like all this energy around you, it expands and grows larger and brighter by the time you come back and you`re better in yourself. `

His wife could hardly believe that he could actually see the energy of her auric outline which had obviously expanded massively under Margaret`s caring hands.

But then Reiki is all about expanding auras or etheric outlines, and this soothing Healer can actually feel the energy of an aura around someone.

Sometimes Margaret can demonstrate to people, such as one particular grandmother, how far out someone`s aura extends. She works with Reiki, the associated guides and also asks Archangels and spirit guides to come in to help at times.

Margaret is intent on ensuring all her patients close down their energy chakras for protection, after every session. Recently when she heard cracking noises from the ceiling and one of her patients felt spaced out after a Reiki session. Margaret put this down to the excitement of disembodied energies who had come in to help with the healing, and had not been sufficiently soothed down and away after the session.

However, this particular gifted Healer does make a particular point of flicking and cleaning off any negative energies which might have erupted and come out during the treatment. She tells me that: `My father was a healer and he also used to flick off the negative energies at the end of the healing sessions, and there was a Jamaican man with us, one time, who could actually see the negative energies as they were flicked away.

You have to get rid of these energies to make sure they are not stuck in your energy fields ~ aura or etheric outline ~ and I myself make a point of smoothing out all the energies after a session. But there was one time when my father was doing his healing work, and my mother was sitting to the side of the patient. After the session he flicked off the negativity, some of which must have gone in her direction and for the next few days she felt very unwell.

`My father, ` Margaret says, `was sometimes helped in his spiritual healing work with an apport which would appear to help him. This was a large piece of ivory shaped like an ancient Chinese man, with a long moustache and beard, holding a long sword. He appeared and came through into physical reality as a gift from the other side when my father was undertaking work in mediumistic circle.

Dad took this piece of ivory along to a museum to be identified and it proved to have been from a Chinese grave, but it seemed to have appeared to help others believe in the energies from the other side which do come in to help. `

Margaret`s husband is more of a psychic who can: `See people as clearly as I`m seeing you, ` he tells me. `Sometimes if they come from long in the past they appear in sepia or in little transparencies. `

And he is often needed to help those on the other side who have become stuck in the earth`s sphere rather than moving on fully on their journey, into the etheric world, because a negative emotion ~ usually guilt ~ is holding them down here. He tells me that these are usually people who have suffered a violent death, he can talk to them and since they are attracted to the light he can ask them to show themselves.

Where Margaret is involved she will bring down the light and say the Lord`s prayer which she describes as a huge mantra. Then she brings in the angels and tells the trapped spirit that `it is all clear now and you need to go on your way. `

When Cyril was in the military police, in Port Said, there was a man who was shot and killed, and once he had sorted him out in the mortuary he said: `If you believe in my ability to contact you where you are now, come and show yourself to me when I return home. ` And, sure enough, this man did appear to him when he arrived back in England.

He goes on to tell me about a certain Ivy Northage who used to be a transfiguration medium and her face used to change to take on the appearance of other spirits. At one time she was in contact with some ladies from an African tribe who used to have many rings to elongate their necks. And right before everyones` eyes Ivy`s neck elongated to take on the shape and form of all those rings around it, and her face changed to adopt the look of a woman from that African tribe.

We discuss all kinds of mediums they have connected with who had almost unbelievable abilities to give exact descriptions to women in the audience to tell of receipts sitting in their handbags, detailing the exact amount of money that had been exchanged. Or otherwise giving descriptions where one woman was slow to recognise the spirit energy that was coming in to connect with her.

The medium, therefore, told her to visualise a certain chest of drawers and to go into one specific drawer on the left of the chest where she would find a book. If she looked on a specific page of the book she would find the name of the person who was trying to make contact with her. This she did and was astounded to find the name of a person who was special to her

When Cyril was in the `specials` during the war, they had been around the area of Friston Forest picking up debris from planes which had crash landed and, about ten years ago, Jill ~ now a friend of Cyril and Margaret ~ was out walking with her brother in the region of Abbotswood, near Friston Forest, on a sparkling frosty morning. Suddenly something on the ground caught her eye and she found a ring which felt important to her.

After this time Jill and Cyril were working in a development class where they were practising psychometry ~ the psychic learning of past events and energies connected with particular treasured items, or jewellery ~ and Jill produced the ring found in Abbotswood.

Now Jill went into a trance with her eyes closed, and Cyril was sitting apart from her and psychically viewing what he could see in connection with the ring. They both found themselves back in the first world war where Jill, in that previous life, had been in the RAF as a pilot and she had been a young very good looking man.

The lady running the development group asked Jill if she could sense any names from the group of RAF colleagues who were surrounding this pilot who had felt such a connection with this ring. They would play for money or for other treasures and on several occasions they were playing to win this particular ring. **This was the same ring as Jill had found in her present existence.**

Jill from her trance state said that she felt she had had the name `Kieran` with a `K` from that lifetime but that there was also another man called Cieran with a `C`. So the development leader asked how many were called Cieran in the group and, to her astonishment, Jill said three and independently ~ from his psychic state ~ Cyril put up three fingers mouthing the number.

But the frustrating thing for Jill, in that past life as Kieran, was no matter how hard she or he tried, the ring was not won.

It seems there is another connection between the two as well because whilst in the present day Jill was with her brother when she found the ring, in this life, through various other psychic journeys Jill and Cyril have found themselves to have been brother and sister previously, in another lifetime entirely.

Endless mysteries and inexplicable happenings appear from the etheric world and it is continually the energy of the Ether which provides the energy source and force for invisible yet very profound healing, using etheric energy in acupuncture, Reiki, cranial osteopathy, homeopathy and spiritual healing.

Chapter Seventeen

Revering the dead in different societies

Sam: Didn`t ancient Egyptians have a belief in the afterlife?

Yes they were very firmly fixed in their rituals and beliefs of what they felt happened after the death of the physical body.

Amidst all of the ceremony and procedures they were not so very far removed from many of our current day beliefs.

Both during life, and after death, they believed in the Ka as the spirit double, etheric body existing around and through everyone. Once a person had died they still believed that the relatives, and loved ones, could be close to the Ka of the recently departed to such an extent that they would write them letters, talk to them, involve them in everything that was currently going on in their lives.

After death they believed that the person, in the shape of his Ba ~ or celestial soul ~ represented and accompanied by the falcon headed God, Horus, had to travel through the Duat on their journey to attain their final aim. This was to reach out and become one with the stars.

On their way through this Duat they would meet up with their fears shaped in the form of their actions and words throughout their lives. Now they would see how they had affected both themselves, and other people, so that if there had been a great deal of negative action and response to their world then they would, it was believed, meet up with all kinds of monsters in this duat underworld.

This journey progresses through twelve gates which echo their perception of the twelve hours of darkness of the night. At this time, the believed, the sun travels under the world before re-emerging on the other side, with the light of the dawn.

The ba or celestial soul would then be faced with the halls of judgement where their actions would be weighed, in the form of their heart ~ as to how much love they had expressed during their lifetime ~ against the feather of the Goddess Ma`at. By now, their heart should be as light and free as a feather, and able to continue, reunited with the Ka or spirit self towards the stars. Here the oversoul, or great Ba, would be waiting to welcome the spirit and individual soul home.

This is very similar to the life review where we have to face the outcome of all our words, actions and intentions, or the karmic repercussions, following our life time in a physical body. The falcon headed Horus accompanies the Ba, or soul, on the journey through the Duat and could be seen as the greater spiritual or oversoul energy, accompanying the individual Ba soul on its journey home.

The Egyptians always believed that the Ba should look to the west, to the God of the west, or Osiris, for guidance from the starting point of this journey. In this way they would be shown the way towards the east, so that the sun would be able to rise again in the dawn.

During life, and beyond, the Egyptians were certain that their Ka etheric double was their spirit energetic body, as we all have when alive in a physical body, and through which we become more of ourselves after we die. But they also believed that the spirit Ka level of being would act as the gateway to reach through to discover and connect with the Ba, or the celestial soul whilst still alive, and that this should be the quest for all of us in life.

There have been all kinds of different types of ancestor worship throughout the ages, through different peoples, and the overall basis is that ancestor worship is based on one idea. The spirit of any ancestor, or person who has died, would still be connected with the family and friends and could still affect the living, possibly even to intercede in spiritual matters.

Therefore the spirit had to be appeased or appreciated in different ways.

An area would often be set aside for the ancestor, an altar erected and offerings of food and drink made, or flowers and material goods to offer comfort in the world beyond. Sometimes there would be photos and letters left asking for wisdom or sharing a joy.

This could be merely a personal connection or a personal altar and reverence for someone who has died, or there could be a special day set aside when all the dead would be honoured and welcomed to return to their tribe, home or place of living.

In Ireland, in ancient times, there is still evidence of their belief in the after life and continuance of the spirit energy through the generations.

In the valley of the Boyne there is a passage tomb, called New Grange, which was originally erected some five thousand years ago. This stone passage tomb is carefully designed to draw the light of the sun at the winter solstice, but also the moon`s light and even the light of Venus along the passageway into the core of the tomb.

At the central core the passage divides into three different chambers at the end, in a cruciform shape of a three leaf clover, with a crescendo and pattern of stones spiralling up above. The people would bring the cremated bones of the recently deceased of their spiritual leaders, and lay them in one of these different sections. In the next section would be either a birthing mother or a newborn child especially chosen to receive the wisdom from the spirit of the recently departed leader. Their energy was believed to still be living in the ether world.

And as the light crept down the passageway the power would be drawn through to connect the two worlds and impart the wisdom of the departed into the newborn, that child would have the opportunity to become the tribe`s spiritual leader later.

Carvings of a triple spiral showing the black and white, white and red and white etheric energies of alchemical transformation ~ from the base through ash to become spiritual ~ appear at the end of the passageway, of this Irish cairn, to signify the actions taking place within the stone carved tomb. The spiral reveals the triple life lived first of all at base level with the earth in the physical life, through the wisdom stages to become immortal beings of light. In fact they may have used New Grange, or Neu Grain as it was called, to cremate the body in the first place in order to capture the wisdom of the spirit energy, immediately, to be passed on to the next generation.

This cairn was constructed in a dome shape, with white quartz on the outside, to attract and reflect the light and to create its own aura or etheric energy field. The inner passageway lifted gently to the cruciform core to draw the light energy inwards in a spiral motion. In the same way light was drawn to the core of anyone inside the passage tomb.

Bronze age man seemed to know about what was happening with the sun and solar winds, and could have specifically designed this tomb to reshape the direction of the life force energy to maintain a balance when the solar wind was decreasing. The extra life force flow would help balance out the increased magnetic field of the earth happening all around them. People would go into the centre of the cairn at times when the solar wind was decreasing to continue to exist. Should we learn from them for our own selves beyond 2012?

When there is a decrease in the solar wind the magnetic field of the earth grows stronger and this negates the normal fertility cycles, so perhaps we should watch out if the solar winds decrease too dramatically in the near future?

I don`t know if you`ve ever been to New Grange, Sam, but it is a fascinating place which creates a very eerie feeling of both life and death when you`re right inside at the top of the passageway. Then they turn out the lights and create the effect of the winter solstice for you. As you watch that light creeping along towards you it is pretty mind blowing.

Sam: No but I`ll definitely go there soon, so is this the only passage tomb of its kind?

Oh no there are many more which were used to draw the etheric light inwards. There is also Knowth and Dowth in the valley of the Boyne, there is Bryn Celli Ddu in Anglesey, Maes Howe in Scotland, and even a small passage tomb on the hill of Tara but there were others in places such as Carnac in France. Here long lines of standing stones portray the path of the spirit on its journey from life, through the stars and beyond into the afterlife world.

They sometimes used these sites as a kind of tomb and had, as at New Grange, a great stone boulder that they would roll across to seal the tomb with themselves inside for a period of up to three days ~ where the light of the winter solstice would be reaching through ~ so that they could lift their light energy and become their etheric double or twin self more fully.

Sam: Hey this is like the resurrection of Jesus.

This could be, Sam, they could have echoed this action.

In his Treatise on Homeopathy Samuel Hahnemann states: `In the state of health the spirit-like vital force (or dynamis) animating the material human organism reigns in supreme sovereignty`. In life we have to keep our ether light energy flowing through us, harmoniously, instead of being battered by a whirlwind of inharmonious negative feelings.

If we can charge up our vital life force through our outer Ka, then we might be able to be in touch more easily both in life and after we leave this mortal coil?

Chapter Eighteen

MESSAGES from THE OTHER SIDE

Sam: I still need to know how it actually feels to die.
I know someone who can tell you this, Sam. Ever since he died at the end of February, 2010, my husband, Peter, has been relaying messages and communicating with me and now I can pass on the answers he has been able to give to me.

`Peter can you now tell me more about the other side of life?`

How it feels to die

There is a great rushing of air as your subtle twin energy body lifts up through the levels and out of the physical body. Immediately any physical sense of weight releases from you.

A gigantic movement of air, a whooshing sound becomes a sigh as human life releases. You are light, no longer held down.

There is confusion, you don`t yet realise you`re going home to reunite with your true soul self, back to where you belong. Your whole energy awareness searches to find some connection or point of context but in between there`s a wave of loving energy sweeping through your etheric being.

A need to reconnect with the familiar known recognised energies yet you find yourself ~ you definitely do still have a `self` ~ aware of everything beyond that logical brain.

Now there`s a sense of power, beyond restriction, a need for readjustment, especially with sudden death as happened to me and my so very sudden departure... for which I am so sorry. This came as a massive shock to you all but is how it had to be.

`But why, why do you have to die so quickly and suddenly?
It is my time, there is so much to do and this is what I have chosen before I ever came in to life. And, as the ending approaches, part of me does know it is about to happen. I have chosen to die at home so I must stop you ringing for help.

Yet my body had been dragging me down for too long, stopping, restricting me and I was losing power. I have to leave, move on to where power and energy are freely available.

The Life Review

Now pulling away from the physical body weight I am not yet free rather impelled to move in a certain direction.

I lift up through layers and levels of light energy, aware of vague shadows or pulls of compulsion, drawn into position, needing to realise some great truths.

I must face my own connection with those shadows before moving on and into layers of intense light energy waiting ahead Now I face results of all my actions, thoughts and intentions

This is the `Halls of Judgement` ~ where actions will be weighed against a feather ~ the life review which must be undertaken by every single soul who dies. I move through at great speed re-experiencing, fully realising the results of situations caused or created by myself in my life just passed.

And how every action has affected not only my true soul but others too. There is realisation of the personal karmic responsibility and how there will be a need to reincarnate again

The soul intentions have to be made clear and higher guidance reaches through with an urge or suggestions of loving forgiveness through the energy though some cannot accept this.

I move through the life review at speed but this is up to the individual. I re-experience in quick succession, images and a whole awareness of all I had done and not done, my intentions, my words which hurt others, how I kept too much emotion locked inside my physical body. Also I know I never managed to share enough of myself which must have been very difficult for all of you who were my family, left behind.

I begin to see how this affected me physically, building up so much resentment and anger inside my poor old body, all of which needed to be released. My life was a permanent struggle in ways I never could understand when physically alive. I release the pain and can also appreciate all the good I have done, my loving generosity and support of all of you.

There can be great darkness and shadows of restriction whilst passing through the light corridor. There must be realisation very tiring for a new-found etheric energy body.

There is no dark tunnel as many perceive as this is only for those who experience the near death situation and offers a turning round point to return to life.

Beyond the review comes total freedom, a surging flowing of lighter frequency energy, altered awareness, realisation and, above all, spirit healing........ in the return to the true soul being.

For me, at this stage, there`s a rush of power everywhere as has never happened in physical life. I welcome this surge of freedom whilst still aware that a great deal of healing waits for me, and that I`m leaving all of you behind.

But the sudden sense of power brings a surge of energy which I use to force and flash that miniature light image into your energy fields. **I have to show I am all right, already healing and becoming my true etheric self which I can show in an image of brilliant white light. This same image appeared before I died and will become this book`s cover.**

Death has to be the ending of the brain`s power but in becoming etheric we gain so much more.

Though there are some souls for whom the time immediately after the enforced life review is bound to bring disorientation and refusal to accept they have died physically.

Ghosts and trapped spirits

A level exists of being half out of the physical half into etheric worlds where what are known as `ghosts` exist. These trapped souls who never manage to move wholly over.

In fact, despite the life review they`re still not wholly

convinced they have died and have no concept about space or time. Instead the life review has caused them to become trapped in a false concept. They still feel able to do something tangible, in the physical world, to overcome their guilt.

They feel this need to return to the earth plane to resolve something and they cannot move on.

They only know that they have a great need to try to make amends and feel, by returning, they are able to do so.

Sometimes the life review feels more as a dream, they cannot accept what has happened. Ghosts are individual energy trapped and pulled down magnetically into the earth`s circumference. The way to release is by love and forgiveness.

The life review began the process ~ as the Duat or negative double world where the Egyptians felt all kinds of monsters could arise ~ and the soul can lack a sense of peace.

The same is true when someone is very angry and feels the manner of their death was unfair and, indeed, a vital part of the whole process of death, and the moving into being a true etheric, lies in being able to release all that has happened.

Otherwise tormented souls are trapped between worlds.

Those on the earth plane can help by sending them through loving forgiveness and light as the whole Ether World IS **the** transporter and transmitter of light which is always healing.

Some have chosen physical suffering as their soul purpose in a specific life so must linger for a longer time in a physically suffering body. Others choose a point in life where they seem, to the outside world, to have everything going for them and yet they choose to exit at this point as their soul has served its purpose..

Look at Princess Diana, she chose to go from her life when she was at her most powerful, and no longer assailed by physical illness, because she wanted and chose to leave a message behind of how to become powerful in life by caring for and about others. Had she lived on she would have

become embroiled in all kinds of difficult circumstances which would have clouded that supreme message. People recognised this true soul purpose in her

I myself chose before my birth and was subconsciously aware of the timing of my death but my concern was for you, my family, that I could not give you warning to ease the pain of the shock when it happened, and also that our son could not be there.

Those who have worn out their spirit light essence of energy ~ having to battle with disease ~ will, once having passed, receive a great deal of help from spirit sources in the Ether World as they deal with the memory of their physical pain.

We come back to the greater part of our soul after physical death, that greater part of ourselves left behind from the moment of physical birth. Immense freedom comes through being reunited with that true part of the self, a luminescent feeling of flow and the chance to regain great levels of wisdom though all wisdom is gained through the light, there are no buildings here.

Reincarnation

Reincarnation into another physical body, through many lifetimes, is part of our process of evolving, re-experiencing and our soul`s growth which comes from the learning involved. Karma is responsible for so much that few realise when they`re alive. It is a person`s karmic legacy which causes all the illnesses and diseases which they have to experience in life.

Arthritis, hereditary diseases ~ look to the karmic legacy which comes through the family DNA. And at some point before we are born we choose the family we will be born into, as well as the people we will meet or connect with as friends, or lovers, in order to be in the right place, at the right time to begin to resolve the karma. We have to re-live and re-experience various different situations and relationships involved with the same soul group to have a chance of the overall karmic release.

We have to experience relationships from every angle, your

grandmother this time could have been your son before. There is no avoiding the results of our previous actions, but we all have ways of finding karmic resolutions..

The multitude of experiences which have to be undertaken and undergone by every soul could never all be experienced in just one lifetime, there is far too much to learn. Therefore every single soul must return until they have finally evolved through the need for any more learning.

Those who commit terrible crimes such as Hitler

There are different levels in the Ether World of energy

When a person dies and becomes wholly an etheric they begin their journey by moving into a specific level of awareness just like Jacob`s ladder in the Bible as is quoted: *`And he dreamed that there was a ladder set up on the earth, and the top of it reached to heaven; and behold, the angels of God were ascending and descending on it.* `

Those who have sinned against humanity, in dire ways, have to exist on the bottom rungs of that ladder which are ~ if you like ~ lower down in the Ether World. Here the capacity to draw in and use light energy is not so great for those who have massive karmic debts to carry through.

But this passage also signifies that every soul in the Ether World will have all the help and guidance they need ~ aka the angels ascending and descending to reach those who are lower down on the ladder of personal realisation and ascension ~ to atone and make amends for what they have done. And in fact the most difficult part of all, for them, will be facing their true self, their oversoul, the core self within and coming to the realisation of just how badly they have acted.

The inner `hell` comes from the realisations which all of us must pass through and those who have committed heinous acts will exist from the time of their life review, until ready to return to the next life, in a different level of energy from that experienced by those more free and enlightened in the Ether World. The victims of their actions, who have also died from physical reality, will be in a different level or area of awareness in the etheric world. But they will also have their own learning to do about why ~ for their own soul growth ~ they caused this crime to be perpetrated against them during their lifetime.

There is always a reason for everything that happens, and the `piper will always have to be paid`. That is what karma is all about but as far as existence in the etheric world is concerned there is perfect justice. For those, such as Hitler, you can be pretty sure that there would have been plenty of inner monsters accosting and assailing him in the duat of the afterlife.

The aim for anyone who becomes wholly their ether self ~ having died from the physical ~ is to move up that ladder of Jacob, in other words to climb higher through the levels of light energy awareness, and wisdom, to be reunited with the higher part of their oversoul. At this stage the need for continued reincarnation no longer becomes necessary.

Existence is a state of becoming and learning, gaining wisdom and light energy through whichever level, dimension or world you currently function.

Suicides

Then there are suicides although those who commit this act do not in fact achieve anything. Their journey through their life review will be that much longer as they must relive through the way they affected other people during life.

They have to remain in that state for a long time when they have committed suicide rather than quickly or relatively easily moving into another level of etheric energy. They have further to climb up the ladder so suicide should never be seen as a solution to anything as this merely prolongs the problem. They will have to come back and do it all over again in a similar way

Chapter Nineteen

Ways to CONTACT those who have died

If we can find the ways and means to connect with the energy of those who have died, this can prove to be a life changing experience, helping find a way through our grief.

The first way to be able to connect with their energy is to be open for signs and coincidences which we normally dismiss.

Find an image of them and talk out loud or talk in your head through your thoughts...........even ask them questions.

Share everything that has recently happened to you. Or write them a letter or an email which you will never send as this is a great way to release all those worries and fears.

Be observant, notice if things, objects or anything moves from its former position unexpectedly. Don`t just put it down to being a lapse in your own memory.

Be aware that any single thing which happens in your life can be a message from her, or him, as can things other people say, especially when you hear something three times.

Also if you want to receive any sign of contact it is vital to stay as positive as possible. Any sign of negativity, despair or self pity immediately forms a blip in your energy field. This makes it much harder for those who have passed on to project their energy through. They exist in a place of wholly positive sheer shining light energy in a fast vibration, they want to shine through your outer energy fields but any signs of negativity will stop this flow of communication.

Listen for sounds or watch for the messages of birds:
A dove signifies peace, a hawk is seeing from above.
An eagle represents power and strength.
A blue jay is a mischief maker, a robin asks to save strength
The owl is often seen after the death of a loved one asking you to learn from your inherent wisdom whilst alive.

A magpie asks you to dig deeper, and a kingfisher asks you to see things differently. The swan is a symbol of transformation

Your sense of touch and the feel of energy is also important. If you feel a waft of air blowing past your face, don`t always dismiss this as the wind. Try not to shut your mind, blocking off all kinds of symbols and signs, let the miracles happen.

That door which opened in front of you, or the knocking on the wall.......this was not the wind. You have to be open to believe in any possibility if you want to come into contact or believe in their continuing energy. They ARE still around and they DO want to reach through to you.

When falling asleep or having just awoken, this is an ideal time for them to make contact with patterns of light that reach through the outer levels of your awareness. And if they can`t reach you any other way they will appear in your dreams.

Light messages are their easiest tool but they need you to receive them. Clear an inner space, be aware of etheric energy existing everywhere, particularly in your own light outline.

Through your outer light fields they can send flashes of light into and through your peripheral vision.

Alter your focus in life away from the normal material and physical reality. Concentrate just beyond normality, look through that other level of energy round that hill or tree.

See how light outlines the whole of your life, especially you as your twinlight self.

The Pharaoh Akhenaten believed so deeply in the Aten sun disc as the source of higher energy, now try feeling or seeing a disc of radiant sunlight right the way round outside your physical shape and form. Set the disc to spin and, immediately, increase the speed of your ether energy.

A way to increase your etheric sight ability is to stare at something, first through one eye and then the other, not by covering the eye but by altering your vision consciousness, this helps you see the other ether level of energy everywhere.

Particular places can be rendolent of their energy, in certain places or at particular times like birthdays and anniversaries it is far easier for them to be in touch with your energy fields

Those who have passed to the other side of life are probably never going to contact us when we expect them to ~ or is this just my husband ~ but if we stay open, observant, attentive and reasonably positive there`s no reason why they won`t come through.

Now I`m about to speak further about my own experiences but I think you have one more question, Sam?

Sam: Are there mechanical means to register other energies?

Yes when we`re talking about things like ghosts then more solid etheric energy collections ~ from the other side of life ~ can be measured by those still living on the earth plane by using EMFs and EVPs.

Electromagnetic field detectors can measure the flow and high frequency of magnetic field changes in the electro magnetic fields.When there is a presence of etheric energy, then the surrounding temperature will drop and the electro magnetic currents are bound to increase.

EVPs ~ electronic voice phenomena ~ measure sounds. Thermal imagers measure in volts/metre the cold spots to capture air movement and electric field readings are able to reveal wave patterns which move around through ether energy. And yet none of these compare to experiencing what you and I have, Sam, in that we KNOW we have been contacted by those who now exist on the other side of life.

Chapter Twenty

My OWN EXPERIENCES

Symbols of synchronicity, patterns, happenings appear in my life after Peter dies on the 26th February, 2010, leaving me convinced he`s still very much here and in contact with me.

I do have to be open to every eventuality but he brings so much comfort to me, at each point of contact, not least as he shows me that he DOES still exist after physical death.

Peter chooses the time of his death very carefully, when our daughter has just arrived back from a holiday in Turkey, some twenty four hours earlier ~ so that she can be with me when he dies. She also still has one month`s tenancy on her cottage, two miles up the road from where I live, which provides us with a bolt hole when I cannot return to our bedroom for a while since this is where he dies. But he knows we will be safe

His symptoms worsen only at the very end so that I do not have time to call the ambulance to get him to hospital, and I take this as a sign that he wants to die at home, and not in the ambulance nor in the hospital.

As previously mentioned, he begins sending white light images of himself through to me six hours after he dies, and the images continue across the next two weeks, sometimes becoming orbs of light which see fit to race around the bedroom at night, always in the dark.

Then of course there are the objects which fly off bookcases, windowsills and across fireplaces. The two books and his keyboard ~ throwing themselves down on the floor in front of me ~ now need an explanation:

One book is A4 size and designed to show how to draw trees. It is opened on a particular page which shows a black walnut tree, very specifically. As I talk about this with a friend she finds, through a book of herbal medicine, the black walnut tree is described as `Jupiter`s nut`. In front of me is a connection between the black walnut tree and the planet Jupiter. Peter wrote four books in his life, one his autobiography and one of them was called: **`The Jupiter Effect`.**

But there is another strange clue on the page about drawing the walnut tree. On one side it mentions: **`outline first with *light* lines`,** at another point it is suggested**: `make a fine faint outlin**e`. A vital message through this book is involved with the twin light outlining self that all of us have. Is Peter already reinforcing this message for me? Of course this twinlight self is vitally our means of departure at the point of death.

The other book he throws down on the floor before me carries a picture on the back of the `Victory` the ship of Nelson

My husband also built model ships, one of them being Nelson`s Victory and now he tells us to throw away this ship.

However his keyboard is interesting. I thought no more at the time of his throwing this object in front of me but several months later, when my own computer crashes, I decide to use Peter`s computer, keyboard and mouse.

He had one of these wireless keyboards and a remote mouse but the keyboard refuses to work. So we take the back off to look at the batteries which are now completely blown and have turned to white acid.

Did he throw that keyboard down in front of me to tell me to replace the batteries before it was too late?

I had been using his mobile phone regularly. On one particular day, some three months after my husband dies, I open up the text messages and all of a sudden the phone flags up a `new message`.

The message comes from the AA and reads: `we are coming out to find and assist you,` but the message is dated at the end of October in 2009, the year before. I do remember around that time that Peter and I had driven out to have a look at the outside lights for the cottage our daughter was about to rent.

He had driven into the drive where the car broke down and refused to start. That was when he called the AA, but why should they be telling me they are coming out to find and assist me some seven months later? Or otherwise why would this message have been stored and refused to appear through his phone? Is this yet another way for Peter to tell me he is still able to find me, to stay in contact, and assist me wherever necessary? He is talking through a machine.

And then there is the lamp. One night, for no accountable reason, a long tubular light ~ filled with water for coloured bubbles to rise ~ just throws itself right over and the water goes everywhere, especially through DVDs and books of Peter`s.

The strange thing is that on the day before I had been rushing around trying to finish off one of my own books to have it published by a particular deadline.

The coincidence in here is that the book I am about to publish has the title: **`A Positive Light Bubble`.** Has Peter thrown that light over for me realise I`ve been rushing around too much, that there`s no panic and it is time to slow down?

Various DVDs and books of his have been drowned in the water of the bubble light falling and they all talk of material things: `The Treasures of the Vatican` and `Millers Antique Guide`. There is a book on `Classic Cars` too. Once again is Peter sending a message through which says that from where he is now, material things have no value?

Whilst we`re mopping up the books, a letter falls out, dated 23rd of March 1991, from the parents of a woman who had been our friend at that time. The letter thanks us for helping her out and being so caring after their daughter`s husband has died.

We had lost contact with this particular friend, Janet, although I did know that she had married again and had met her next husband, Mike, on several occasions. So that in finding this letter in November 2010, I feel I have to phone to tell her about what I have found.

She answers by saying: `How did you know?`

It turns out that her second husband, Mike, has just died suddenly and unexpectedly, and she feels that life is being extremely unfair that it should happen to her all over again.

Then she proceeds to tell me that the funeral will be on the following Friday. HAS PETER THROWN THIS LETTER AT ME JUST IN TIME TO ATTEND A FUNERAL I WOULD HAVE KNOWN NOTHING ABOUT OTHERWISE?

I have to proceed to sort out the necessary paperwork after Peter has died and thought I knew where everything was, and that I had filed away all the necessary documents. I know I had checked them carefully.

Then the date of June 2010 ~ which would have been our forty fourth wedding anniversary ~ is approached by me with some trepidation on my part, and great feelings of sadness.

However, just the day before the date of our anniversary a premium bond win arrives, in Peter`s name. Not an enormous win but enough to go out for a meal on the day that would have been special to us ~ perfect timing as a present for me.

I had no idea there were even any premium bonds in his name, still in existence. I hadn`t seen any certificate when I went through the paper work. And yet now, suddenly, the certificate in his name suddenly appears in a pile of paperwork, out of the blue.

Obviously I send this back to the premium bond people and, once again with perfect timing, £5000 comes through to me, from Peter, for my birthday.

So now he has given me both an anniversary and a birthday present from where he is. His timing is immaculate.

One night he sends me through a very strong image of the

eye of a tiger and also a picture of our garden although I can`t understand why. Then I remember that Peter`s wedding ring had carried a tiger`s eye stone ~ he seldom wore this ring which is why I had forgotten ~ and I had buried this ring in the earth, in the garden, after he died to clean it.

This all happens the day before I am due to see our son and convinces me that Peter wants me to unearth and clean this ring so that our son can have it which I can now do.

One day, as I am walking up the stairs, I can feel him walking up those stairs alongside of me. When we reach the top the door ~ which was closed ~ suddenly opens and encourages me to walk into the room. There is no wind at all, and no sign of anything to open the door, other than him.

At a different time his portrait jumps off the wall of his one time study and hits our daughter on the shoulder when she`s been at her computer, on his desk, generally overworking. Is this his message to tell her to stop?

A clock resting on the windowsill with his picture lying alongside, suddenly throws both itself and the picture down on the floor sending the batteries flying out of the clock.

When he died he had left a piece of his music open on the piano at the page where the song was entitled: `I`ll know`. Well he does now.

At another time we find a small dictaphone machine of his carrying his voice singing a song from My Fair Lady with the words: `not long now until it is goodbye. `

On another occasion I find an unnamed tape which I decide to play in my car`s cassette player ~ which I no longer have ~ and when I push the tape in, whilst driving to work, I`m suddenly aware of his voice practising to sing for an opera. His lovely tenor voice is singing: `I am happy, happy, happy. `

However, the next part of the tape moves on to his singing of the words: `I am sad, sad, sad.` At this point I eject the tape and proceed to work. But I must have pushed the tape in again before I switch off the car that night.

The next day I jump into the car to go shopping, try to switch on the engine and nothing happens. There is no sign of life at all and I leave the car and take the bus.

My daughter says she`ll have a go at starting the car, she tries the ignition which splutters and dies. Then, for some reason, she ejects the tape and tries again and the car starts perfectly. Obviously, Peter does not want me to hear his singing words of sadness. Anyway I now know, from all of his messages, that he is elated to be free in the Ether World. Another time I definitely feel Peter stroke my arm.

On a night when our daughter has been particularly upset about her father and I come upstairs worrying about her, he blows on my face not once but twice which is very comforting and helps prove that he is watching over us and still cares.

The day before what would have been his seventieth birthday, in January 2011, she finds a letter amongst some items which had not been in her possession for many years. This letter is dated way back at the end of the nineteen nineties, is from her father at a time when she`d been at university, at a time we were doing the worried parents bit.

But Peter has never been one to express his feelings or outwardly show his concern, certainly not in a letter. And yet on this day ~ the day before the one we have both been dreading because of his birthday ~ this letter appears and expresses concern for her in all kinds of ways, even giving her a nickname which is extremely comforting and so unlike him.

Curiously, even before he died, on his birthday January 17th 2010, we had arranged to go to a film and to have a meal which would be something I really looked forward to doing. However, on this day, I found myself overtaken by a deep and totally unreasonable, out of character inexplicable anger rising inside of me....but why? Was this because I already knew this was to be his last birthday whilst still alive?

The very strange thing is that we manage to get through the 17th of January 2011 without too much sadness, this time, and yet with my remembering the anger I had felt the year before on his birthday.

However, back on January 18th, 2010, the day after Peter`s last birthday alive, we had to attend the funeral of my aunt and, once again, this made me unbelievably angry. *Why on earth should I feel such anger at a funeral? Did part of me know this would be the last funeral I would attend before Peter`s?*

And lo and behold, the day after his would be birthday in *2011,* at exactly the same date, time and place ~ apart from the year ~ that my aunt had been buried the year before, now her niece has her own memorial service in the same church in 2011, again at eleven am, on the 18th January, in the same place, Chiddingstone, Kent.

This proves to be too much of a coincidence and holds too many memories which unsettles me more than a little.

There had been several strange happenings before Peter died so suddenly and unexpectedly ~ not least the cover photo taken six months before he died, and I should now speak of the tulips

Five days before he would die so suddenly I asked my husband to buy me some white flowers. He came back with red and yellow tulips! I told him, quite emphatically, that I did not like tulips since they never lasted for long and normally just bent over and died within a week.

However, those tulips not only outlasted him, defiantly surviving for four weeks, but they continued to stand straight upwards without any inclination to bend over. Afterwards, I planted them in the garden where they continued to take their straight up stance. *Was this already a message from him that life does go on and that none and nothing can ever die?*

Of course I was inundated with white flowers when he died

Strangely, some five months after my husband died, I gave a friend a bunch of cut flowers ~ chrysanths ~ for her birthday. Three weeks later, as she was throwing them away, she noticed one was not only still very much alive ~ white of course ~ but actually growing roots. Cut flowers don`t do that when they`ve had the stem broken off and this one lasted for three months.

Yet another message from Peter that life goes on?

Seven months before he died he insisted on my having my astrological horoscope done, by a friend of our daughter, as a birthday present. What came out was as follows:**TRANSITING CHIRON OPPOSITION NATAL VENUS** *Entering 4 Mar 2010, exact 19 Mar2010, leaving 5Apr 2010, entering 5Aug2010, exact 25 Aug 2010*

Your relationship with your partner is a source of pain either through your partner`s actions or an external event. You have the opportunity now to heal the past and move forward.

This transit can be linked to emotional pain but it is also possible that your partner is suffering from a physical illness. Either way it is important to nurture yourself and loved ones. It is vital you treat yourself kindly as this can be an acutely painful time. Tears may flow but it is ultimately a time of healing and education. In some cases it is possible that your partner is undergoing a transformation, clearing out old emotional wounds from the past to positively affect your present life.

We had no idea that Peter had any serious disease and his death came as a total shock, out of the blue.

Curiously, I had booked for him to have his own reading undertaken one week after he died ~ what would it have shown

Shortly after Peter`s death we find a calender which has been on his desk and, at the time when he dies, this is on the page showing the days from January through to March in 2010.

Every day of the months of January and March are shown in grey, however February is shown in pink as though leading up to something, and the dates of the 26th and 27th ~ he died on the night in between ~ are printed in bright red as if to say:`danger` This is a pre printed calender, nothing was written or drawn on it by any of us, but it is shouting out a warning to us all.

Once or twice I ask Peter for proof he is still around.

One time I ask him for a sign such as something moving and immediately the shadow of a bird passes across the skylight window and reflects across his portrait on the wall.

The next time I ask him for a sign to confirm a question I have asked him, I suggest the noise of a bang from outside in connection with a car going past or somesuch, or otherwise for the lights to flicker. He never has done anything to order and nothing happens. Two hours later, about 11.30 pm there is a sudden loud bang which comes from outside, not once but twice to reinforce the message. I never do find out what this is.

Another time when I suggest he hasn`t been around so much lately he immediately moves my hairdryer, not once but twice and I can hear it moving along the wall from behind the cupboard, immediately beneath a photo of Peter.

Our son`s book had been due to be published with a one week window before publication. This turns out to be the week Peter chooses to die so our son is able to dedicate this book to his father, just before going to print and on sale.

On the date of the anniversary of the one year since he died ~ once again a day I am not looking forward to ~ my daughter and I go out for the day. Her car keeps overheating and running out of water from the radiator. We become involved in several distracting activities during the day and by 6pm ~ the time I was dreading happening as an echo of the year before ~ we find ourselves opposite the wonderful Hotel du Vin in Tunbridge Wells.

We cannot go on and go home ~ which is not where I want to be anyway at this time ~ because the car needs to cool down before we can add water to the radiator. Therefore we decide there is nothing else for it but to go across the road and have a drink in the hotel. Whilst I am standing at the bar ordering the drinks, Peter definitely comes up to the bar behind me and I can almost lean back against his soothing presence, he touches my shoulder, I hear his voice but noone is there when I turn round.

Yet I feel that he has even been responsible for the car overheating to distract us away from reliving our memories of the dreaded time a year before. Of course the car is fine the next day with no loss of water from the radiator!

Earlier on this day, when I am in a beautiful place at Scotney Castle, in Kent, down by the lake by the old castle, I ask him out loud: `Are you here Peter?` And the answer I receive: `Oh yes I am!` is so loud and so defiantly given in the subtle tones of his own voice that I am completely reassured.

I don`t see him in the way everyone expects to see someone after they`ve died ie just exactly as they were when in a physical body. Rather, he keeps giving and showing me the message that he is now in his etheric shape and form ~ a shape and form he had already shown to me before he died!

It is a fact that when someone has died they are close and more able to be contacted by us when we need them, particularly on those anniversaries and birthdays.

Their energy comes in more closely to be around in our energy fields at this time.

Not long after he died I had been holding a conversation with Peter, in my head, and bemoaning the fact that when he was alive he always intended to pull off that one miracle. He was an author too, and always said he would be able to appear in a publisher`s office, spontaneously, to show them a book.

But he died and never achieved this, I say: `Oh Peter now you can`t ever pull off that one big miracle, can you? `
And his voice shouts out in my head: `Oh yes I can! `

And it is only now, over a year since he died, I can finally see what he means as this book is about to be published, carrying an ethereal image of him on the cover out to the world, to prove we DO all exist, with our outlining twin, whether alive or after we`ve died!

Now he has HIS miracle! He showed me the same image before and just after he died, and now this image WILL appear in a publisher`s office and everywhere on this book!

Some five or six years ago Peter used to own a dark blue lambretta which looked just the same only he had to sell his beloved scooter because he was too cold in the winter riding it around and had to succumb to owning a car with a heater like the rest of us. He always said that when he was on his lambretta he could kid himself he was in the south of France riding along the mountain roads from one beach to another which was where he always ideally wanted to be.

He doesn`t need the scooter to be there now but it is still waiting there on the road, some three days later, not abandoned by anybody but rather as a symbol, I think, for me.

He shines so many shapes and images of light on my wall, from a pair of glasses, to a trumpet, even to an image like a shroud that is filled with white light and radiates white light all around. Yet again proof of him as not being buried in the ground but he is showing me that his energy is still all around, everywhere, moving in etheric levels of energy.

I see images of people which reflect from him through the light on the wall and, shortly after he died when I was repainting the wall, the image of a man with a child in front of him insisted on appearing through the paint.

His portrait is on the wall and light strands flicker across his face to reflect the beautiful place where he`s now chosen to be.

In fact he has been talking to me right the way through this book and he has, each time, advised me in which way I should progress with the chapters, urging me to talk of electromagnetism and that super charged force of energy which is now the Magni force. Also, of course, the likeness of the ether`s energy to snow and the reason for the common cold, but most of all about the etheric world from where all his communications with me have come.

In every way shape and form this man has continued to explain and demonstrate to me that he is still very much aware and existing in his ether light body as an individual presence and essence of energy. There is no way that any of us ever dies completely.

At *the point of death you jump, leap, are pushed or pulled by an unresisting force which releases you from your physical form, and you claim an immediately faster finer vibrational frequency. Physical boundaries which once held you suddenly release and for those left behind there seems to be an impenetrable breach. However, those who have passed over to the other side of life want to reassure us all of their continuing existence.*

And still the contact from his other world continues even surrounding my name. On one particular Tuesday I go to visit a very clever esoteric numerologist to ascertain which name I should use for putting this book out to the world.

She confirms to me that I should bring back and incorporate my maiden name along with my married name and she has brought back my memories of the Wilson family for me.

On the following day I attended a Spiritualist church for the first time and towards the end of the session the medium declares: `somebody is playing the drums loudly in my ear.`

This has to be my husband, Peter, who was playing the drums

on the night we met. She describes him in all kinds of ways as being a great drummer and then says there is an older woman and man whom he now brings forward.

The woman has a look of me and is a kind caring person and both of them are raising their glasses to an anniversary. Then the medium describes: `they are both saying they are so proud of you, ` I guess for writing this book and bringing forward the information which this book contains.

These are my parents, Mr and Mrs Wilson ~ my mother died forty years ago almost to the day of this happening and my father twenty years ago ~ and, astonishingly, this all happens just before the date that would have been Peter`s and my forty fifth wedding anniversary!

But the surprises are set to continue..............

On the actual day that would have been our forty fifth anniversary, I was feeling sad because Peter was not with me.

In the evening my daughter had requested that we unearth some old photos of the house she grew up in. The very first folder of photos which I opened revealed a party we had held for our silver wedding anniversary.

And then, unbelievably, a photo reveals itself, a photo which I had thought I had thrown away since it had so unnerved me when it was originally taken, in August 2009!

The photo which has now appeared specifically to form the front cover of this book!

Here he is, familiar cigar in hand, but this man when he died had a little hair that was all dark and certainly did not have a white beard. This photo cannot have been over exposed, the leaves would not be green, hand in flesh colour, cigar brown.

He is appearing on the day that would have been such a special anniversary for us ~ in his ether double body.

A photo of my parents, glass in hand, sits on the mantlepiece and I realise it is taken on their anniversary too!

Addendum 30th June 2011

There was a situation lingering at the time of Peter`s death and I seek to resolve this finally. Peter had fallen out with his sisters about a family inheritance and I would like to prove that they never intended what happened eventually.

I decide to go to see the man who was his accountant way back in the 1990s when the beginnings of the problem emerged, and before I go I write a predictive letter on my computer which I intend to send to the sisters if all goes to plan

I save this letter as a file on my computer and ask Peter to let me know, in the next hour, whether I am doing the right thing, to give me a sign. I ask for something obvious like a flash of light but of course he never does anything to order.

I turn off the machine and have my lunch and when I come back, an hour later, I switch on to find that the particular document file with his sister`s name on it is now surrounded by about twelve empty temporary files, how strange.

I go to see the guy in the evening but nothing works out and I have no way to resolve the situation on a material level.

The next day, as I am deleting the letter which could never be sent, along with all of those temporary files, its as if Peter is telling me: `I put up all those temporary files around the letter to show you it wouldn`t work, you couldn`t send that letter out ~ it was only on your computer temporarily ~ but thank you for trying. `

Peter Eynon Smart has shown me, in so many ways, that we DO ALL continue to live in our own ether light body, after we die from our physical existence. Now he, and I, can only hope that this book will offer to you the chance to believe in this secret of immortality too?

The energy lives on

....